OXFORD
UNIVERSITY PRESS

Tracey Gibbins

Blue Dot 1

Workbook

1. Who are you? 2
2. What is your identity? 11
3. What makes a group's identity? 20
4. What size is a community? 29
5. Why do we need communities? 38
6. How can communities make our lives better? 47
7. How do we celebrate our culture? 56
8. Where do we experience culture? 65
9. Why is learning about other cultures important? 74
10. How do people communicate? 83
11. Why do living things communicate? 92
12. What do people and animals communicate through their senses? 101
13. What patterns can people make? 110
14. What patterns are there in nature? 119
15. Why are patterns important? 128
16. How can change happen? 137
17. Who can make things change? 146
18. How does change affect us? 155

Writing Resource 164

1 Who are you?

A Look and write the letter.

1 name   f
2 brother   __
3 friend   __
4 animal   __
5 school   __
6 sister   __

B Complete the chart.

doll   pizza   ~~burger~~   video game

Food	Toys and Games
burger	

A Circle the correct option.

1 I **am** / **is** eight years old.

2 They **are** / **is** my friends.

3 It **am** / **is** a burger.

4 I like Arzu. We **am** / **are** friends.

5 This **are** / **is** my sister, Emma.

6 My favorite colors **are** / **is** red and blue.

B Complete the sentences.

1 _____ I'm _____ seven years old.

2 _______________ ten years old.

3 _______________ nine years old.

4 _______________ seven years old.

1 I am not   **a** He isn't

2 It is not   **b** It isn't

3 They are not   **c** You aren't

4 You are not   **d** She isn't

5 He is not   **e** I'm not

6 She is not   **f** They aren't

D Complete the sentences with the correct form of *be*.

1 They _____aren't_____ sisters.

2 He _____________ a doll.

3 It _____________ an animal.

4 They _____________ brothers.

5 It _____________ a burger.

6 She _____________ the teacher.

A Look at the pictures. Who do you think the personal profiles are about? Circle.

Two brothers   Two sisters   Two friends

Who are we?

My name is Sara.
I'm eight years old.
I like burgers.
I like animals.
My favorite color is blue.

My name is Layla.
I'm seven years old.
I like pizza.
I don't like dolls.
My favorite color is pink.

We live in Egypt.
We go to school together, and we like it.
We aren't sisters. We're friends!

 Underline these words in the text.

name   burgers   animals   pizza   dolls   school   sisters   friends

 Circle *True* or *False*.

1 Sara is eight years old.   (True)   **False**
2 Sara likes burgers.   **True**   **False**
3 Layla is eight years old.   **True**   **False**
4 Layla likes dolls.   **True**   **False**
5 Sara and Layla live in Mexico.   **True**   **False**
6 Sara and Layla go to school together.   **True**   **False**

 Look and match.

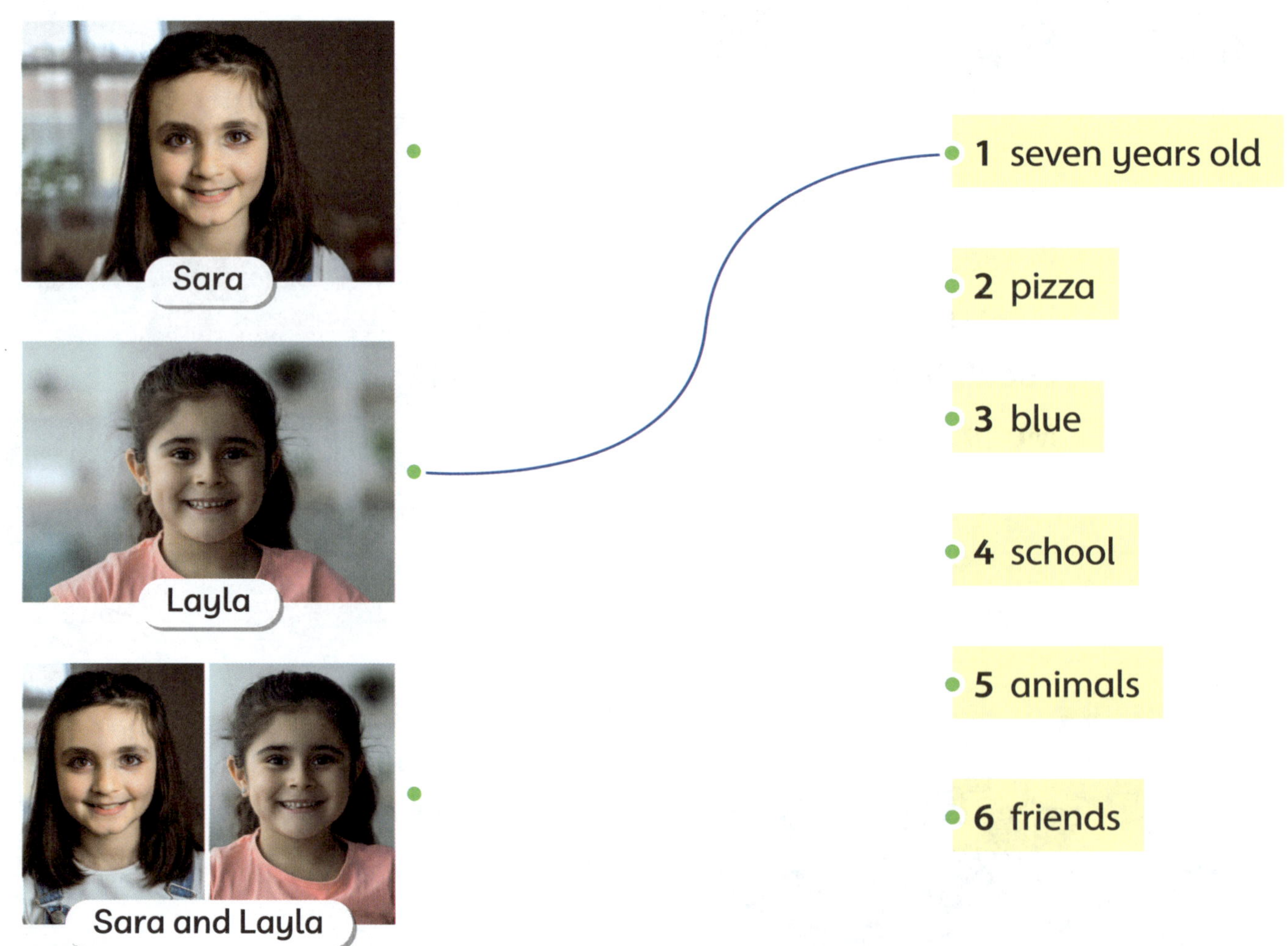

A Circle the correct option.

1 (**blond**) / **different**

2 **color** / **fingerprint**

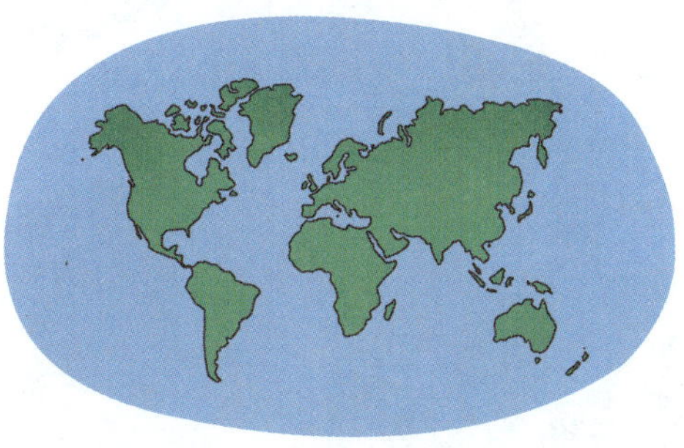

3 **blond** / **world**

4 **fingerprint** / **same**

5 **color** / **world**

6 **different** / **same**

B Complete the sentences.

> different   blond   fingerprints   ~~same~~   color

1 The brothers have the _______ **same** _______ eye color. They have blue eyes.

2 My sister has _______________ hair.

3 All the people in the world have different _______________.

4 My favorite _______________ is green.

5 My favorite food is pizza. My sister has a _______________ favorite – burgers!

A **Look and write the letter.**

1 children   <u>b</u>
2 do gymnastics   __
3 draw   __
4 fly   __
5 love   __
6 read   __

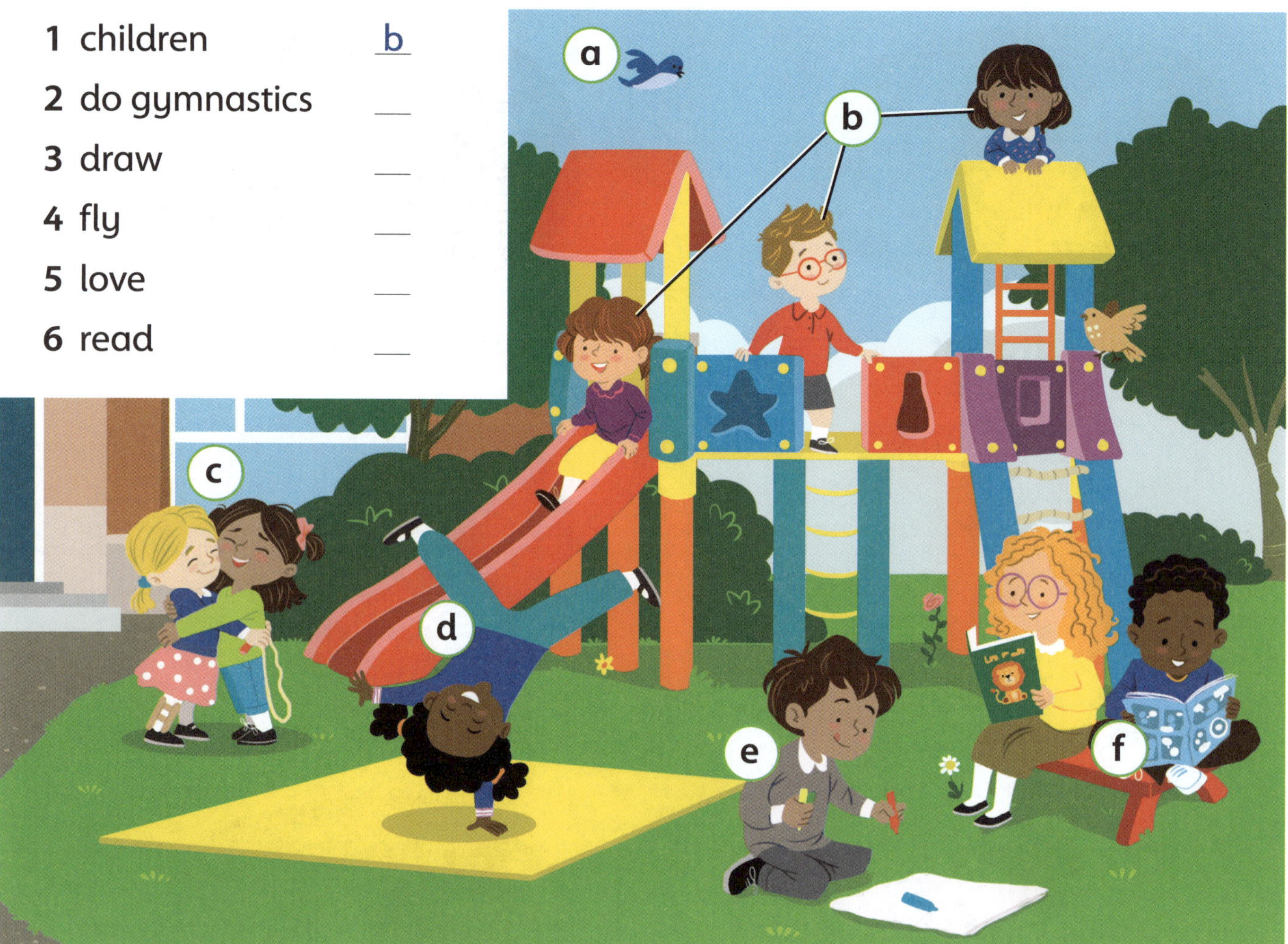

B **Circle the correct option.**

1 Gabriel likes **flying** / **reading** books about animals.
2 Joanna likes **doing gymnastics** / **drawing** pictures of her family.
3 Simon wants to **fly** / **love** around the world.
4 The **children** / **draw** have different fingerprints.
5 Amaka likes to **children** / **do gymnastics** on Wednesdays.
6 Hiroto **loves** / **reads** the color blue.

C **Which words in A are things a person does?**

<u> do gymnastics </u> , _________________ , _________________ ,

_________________ , _________________

1 Word Study

A Check (✓) the nouns.

1 ✓ a teacher
2 ☐ like
3 ☐ a color
4 ☐ a girl

5 ☐ a ball
6 ☐ a fire station
7 ☐ a brother
8 ☐ same

B Match.

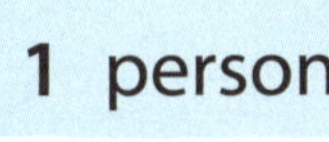

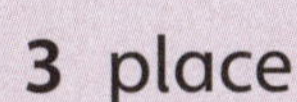

a boy

school

a book

the world

a fingerprint

Dad

C Complete the sentences.

> Mexico   friend   cake

1 I like ________________ . (a thing)
2 I like my ________________ . (a person)
3 I like ________________ . (a place)

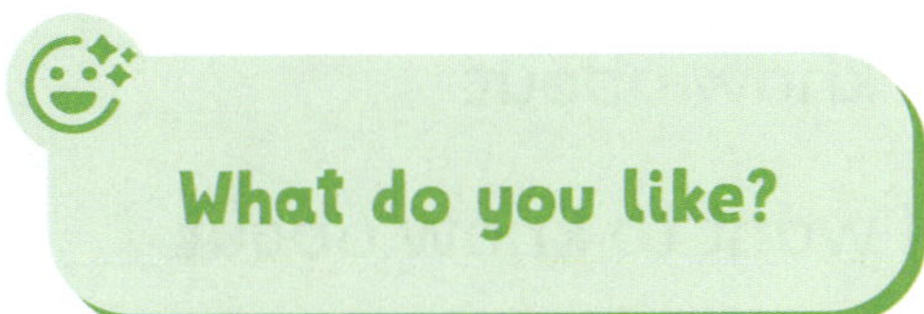

What do you like?

A Complete the chart.

burger   video game   pizza   ~~brother~~   friend   doll   children   sister

Person	Thing
brother	

B Complete the sentences with the correct form of *be*.

1 She's________ blond. ✓

2 It ________ an animal. ✗

3 They ________ the same color. ✓

4 It ________ a school. ✓

5 They ________ sisters. ✗

6 We ________ friends. ✓

Unit 1 and Me

My learning in this unit

I know about ____.

I want to know about ________________________________.

2 What is your identity?

A Look and write the letter.

1 daughter   <u>a</u>

2 pilot

3 mom

4 dad

5 grandma

6 grandpa

7 dentist

B Match.

1 mom   a husband

2 grandma   b son

3 daughter   c grandpa

4 wife   d dad

A Check (✓) the correct question.

1 ☐ **A:** What is it?
   ✓ **A:** What are they?

B: They're pencils.

2 ☐ **A:** What is it?
   ☐ **A:** What are they?

B: It's a tooth.

3 ☐ **A:** What is it?
   ☐ **A:** What are they?

B: They're planes.

4 ☐ **A:** What is it?
   ☐ **A:** What are they?

B: It's a ball.

B Complete the questions.

1 Lucie: _____Who is_____ he?
Adem: He's my dad, Ata.

2 Lucie: ______________ they?
Adem: They're my friends, Sung-ho and Elias.

3 Lucie: ______________ she?
Adem: She's my grandma, Zeynep.

4 Lucie: ______________ she?
Adem: She's my mom, Fatma.

5 Lucie: ______________ they?
Adem: They're my sisters, Nuray and Gamze.

 Circle the correct option.

1 **Louis:** (**Who**) / **What** is she?
   Emilia: She's my mom.

2 **Louis:** **Who** / **What** is it?
   Emilia: It's a cake.

3 **Louis:** **Who** / **What** are they?
   Emilia: They're my brothers.

4 **Louis:** **Who** / **What** are they?
   Emilia: They're photos.

5 **Louis:** **Who** / **What** is he?
   Emilia: He's my grandpa.

6 **Louis:** **Who** / **What** are they?
   Emilia: They're my friends.

 Complete the questions and answers.

1 **A:** _____Who are_____ they?
   B: _____They're_____
   Naomi's family.

2 **A:** _______________ it?
   B: _______________ a photo.

3 **A:** _______________ she?
   B: _______________
   Bashir's grandma.

4 **A:** _______________ they?
   B: _______________ planes for
   the pilots.

A Look at the pictures. What do you think the story is about? Circle.

Two sons   A grandma and grandpa   A family

My Special Brother and Sister

Ayla is showing photos to her class.

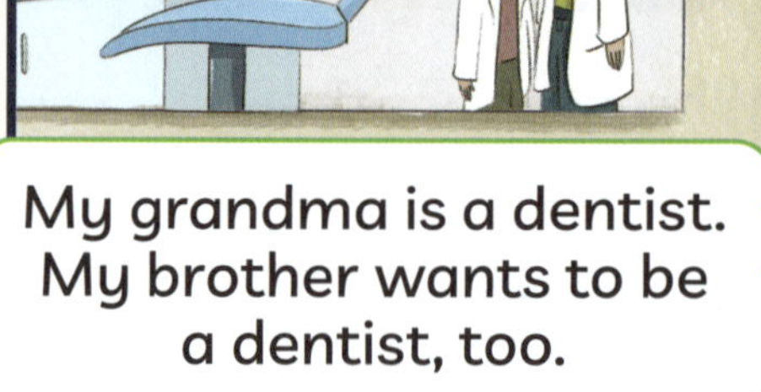

Underline these words in the text.

grandma   dentist   dad   pilot

Match.

1 Mert

2 Elif

a 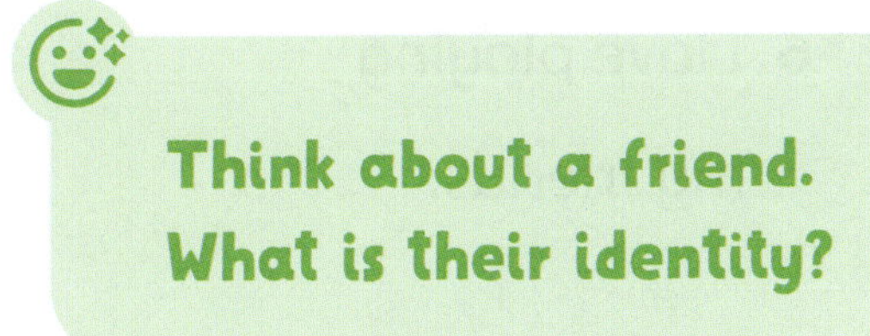

b

c

d

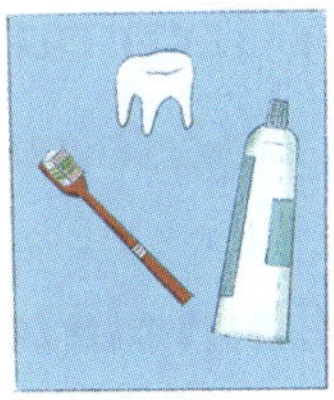

e

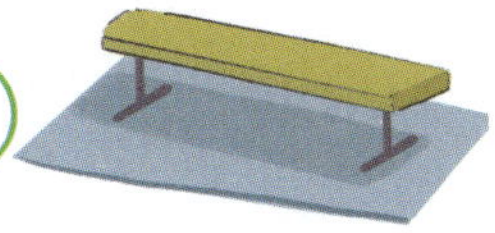

f

Circle the correct option.

1 Ayla is showing **photos** / **pilots** to her class.

2 Mert is **nine** / **ten** years old.

3 Ayla's **brother** / **grandma** is a dentist.

4 Ayla's **dad** / **grandma** is a pilot.

5 Ayla loves her **brother and sister** / **friends**.

Think about a friend. What is their identity?

A Circle the correct option.

  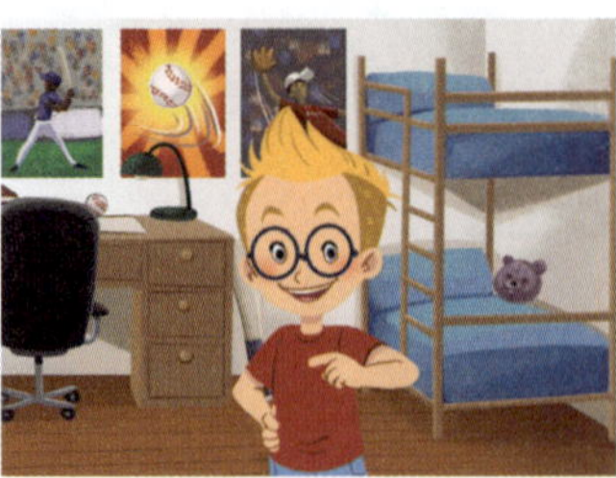

1 This is Tommy's **baseball** / **bedroom**.

2 He likes the **bike** / **violin**.

3 His favorite **student** / **T-shirt** is red.

4 Tommy loves playing **baseball** / **the violin**.

5 His **bedroom** / **bike** is green.

6 He's a **student** / **T-shirt**.

B Complete the sentences.

student   baseball   violin   bedroom   bike   T-shirt

1 I have a blue _____ T-shirt _____ .

2 I love my green _______________ .

3 I like listening to the _______________ .

4 I'm a _______________ , and my favorite class is English.

5 What's this? It's my _______________ .

6 I love playing _______________ with my friends.

What's in your bedroom?

A **Look and write the letter.**

1 calm   <u>a</u>

2 kind   ___

3 friendly   ___

4 funny   ___

5 duck   ___

6 spider   ___

B **Write the letters to complete the words in the sentences.**

1 Hileni is <u>f</u> u <u>n</u> <u>n</u> y and f __ i __ __ **dl** __. People like her.

2 Hileni is __ __ **nd**. She loves her friends and family.

3 Hileni is **c** __ __ **m**. She likes to read in the park.

4 She sees a __ **p** __ **d** __ __ and a __ **uc** __ in the park.

A Check (✓) the correct option.

1 a ☐ leo
b ☑ Leo

2 a ☐ france
b ☐ France

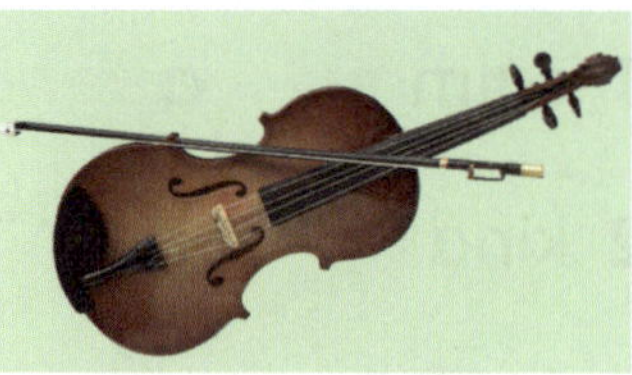

3 a ☐ violin
b ☐ Violin

4 a ☐ sister
b ☐ Sister

5 a ☐ lucie
b ☐ Lucie

6 a ☐ japan
b ☐ Japan

B Complete the chart.

friend   ~~canada~~   family   tommy   duck   egypt

Capital Letter	No Capital Letter
Canada	__________
__________	__________
__________	__________

C Read and complete. Use capital letters for countries and people's names.

pablo   ~~eight~~   pilot   spain   carmen

This is Vicente. He's ¹____eight____ years old.
He lives in ²________________ . He's standing with
his mom, ³________________ , and his dad,
⁴________________ . His mom is a ⁵________________ .

A **Write the words in the correct groups.**

funny   daughter   ~~grandpa~~   bike   dentist

1 dad, son, _____grandpa_____
2 mom, grandma, _____________
3 pilot, teacher, _____________

4 calm, friendly, _____________
5 baseball, doll, _____________

B **Complete the questions and answers.**

1 A: _____Who's_____ she?
   B: _____She's_____ Jane.

2 A: _____________ they?
   B: _____________ Jane's parents.

3 A: _____________ he?
   B: _____________ her husband.

4 A: _____________ it?
   B: _____________ a spider.

5 A: _____________ they?
   B: _____________ ducks.

Unit 2 and Me

My learning in this unit

I know about ____.

I want to know about ____.

3 What makes a group's identity?

A **Look and write the letter.**

1 beach   _e_

2 eat   __

3 laugh   __

4 swim   __

5 make sandcastles   __

B **Read and complete.**

uncle   cousin   watch TV   holiday   aunt

I'm Marcia. This is my family. My mom is Rosa. Ricardo is my mom's brother. That means he's my **1** _____uncle_____. His wife Amy is my **2** _______________. They have a daughter, Lena. She's my **3** _______________. My family likes to have a party when there is a **4** _______________. We have fun. Then we **5** _______________ at the end of the day.

Grammar

A **Circle *True* or *False*.**

1 There is one daughter.

True   **False**

2 There's one student.

True   **False**

3 There is a husband.

True   **False**

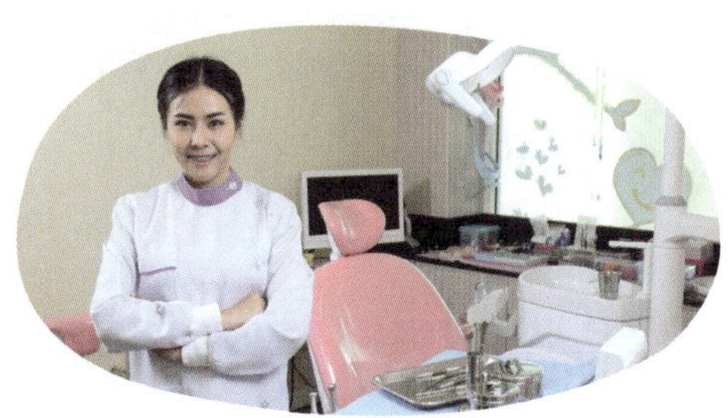

4 There's a dentist.

True   **False**

B **Check (✓) *Yes* or *No*.**

1 There are two teachers.

☐ Yes   ☑ No

2 There are two students.

☐ Yes   ☐ No

3 There are schools.

☐ Yes   ☐ No

4 There are bikes.

☐ Yes   ☐ No

5 There are three dolls.

☐ Yes   ☐ No

 Complete the sentences with *There's* or *There are*.

1 ___There are___ five friends.

2 _______________ a grandma.

3 _______________ one teacher here.

4 _______________ a new student.

5 _______________ two sons.

6 _______________ pilots on the plane.

 Complete the sentences.

1 ___There are four___ spiders.

2 _______________ _______________ sandcastle.

3 _______________ _______________ beach.

4 _______________ _______________ cousins.

5 _______________ _______________ cake.

6 _______________ _______________ balls.

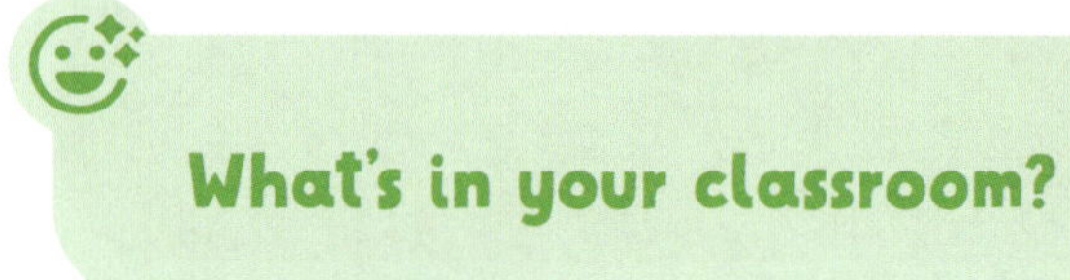

A **Read the story. What is it about? Circle.**

A family at home   A family on a holiday   Children playing games

A Day With Our Family

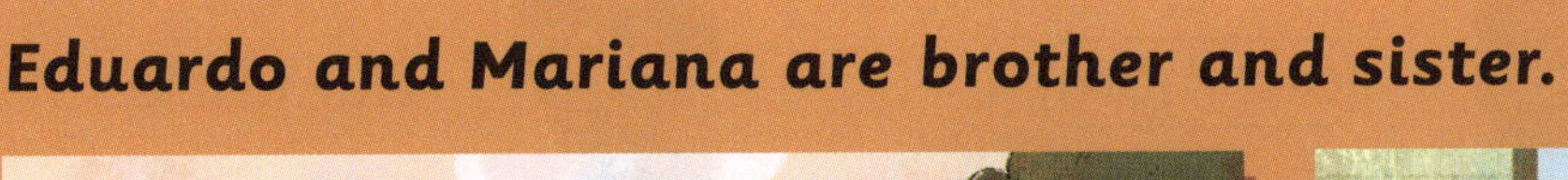

Eduardo and Mariana are brother and sister.

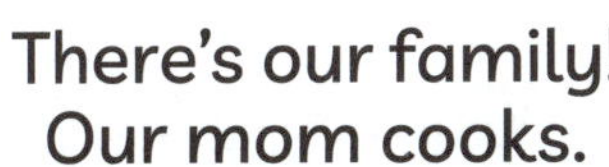

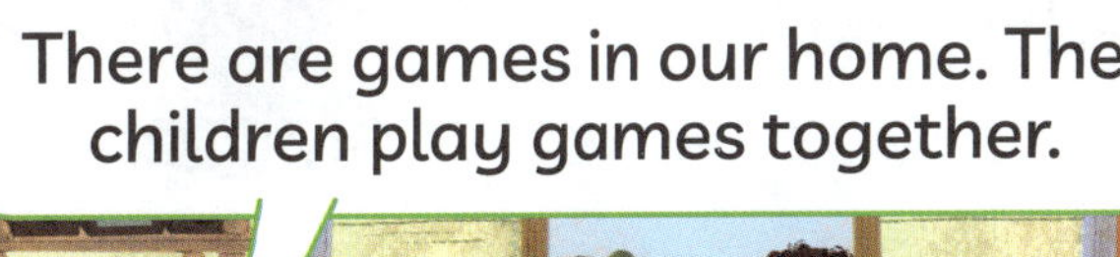

 Underline these words in the text.

C **Contrast the people. Circle the answer.**

1 Who cooks?  (our mom)    our uncle

2 Who eats?  our mom    our uncle

3 Who watches TV?  our dad    our aunt

4 Who reads?  our dad    our aunt

5 Who plays games?   the children     the parents

6 Who talks?   the children     the parents

D **Complete the sentences.**

1 Eduardo is Mariana's _____brother_____ .

2 Eduardo and Mariana have two _____________ .

3 Eduardo and Mariana's dad _____________ .

4 There are _____________ in the home.

5 Eduardo and Mariana love their _____________ .

A Look and write the letter.

1 coach __b__   3 team ____

2 cheer   4 uniform

B Write the letters to complete the words in the sentences.

1 Kate, Valentina, and Malaika are a __g__ r __o__ __u__ p of friends.

2 They play s __ c __ __ r together.

3 Their __ __ am is called The Ducks.

4 They wear yellow u __ __ f __ __ ms.

5 They have a good __ oa __ __.

A Circle the correct option.

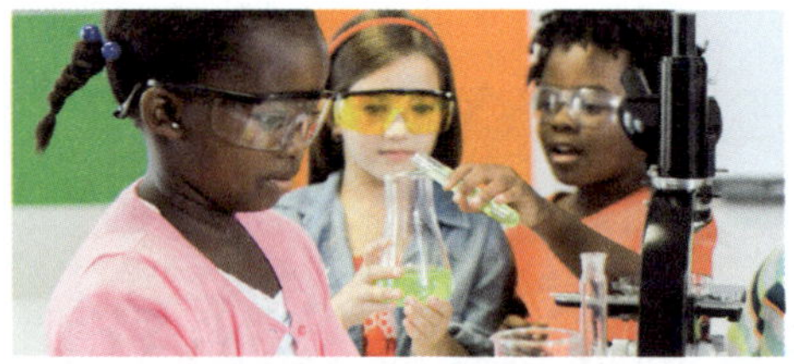

1 They go to a **chess** / **club**
on Wednesdays.

2 She loves **art** / **ballet** club.

3 He likes **ballet** / **chess** club.

4 Their favorite club is
art / **chess** club.

5 They **make friends** / **learn**
at school.

6 They **learn** / **make friends**
in the classroom.

B Complete the sentences.

~~art~~   chess   makes friends   ballet

1 Simon goes to _____art_____ club
on Mondays.

2 He goes to ___________ club
on Tuesdays.

3 On Wednesdays, he goes to
___________ club.

4 Simon ___________ in his clubs.

Word Study

A Write the verbs.

1 She reads a book.

reads

2 They like soccer.

_____

3 He draws a picture.

_____

4 They learn ballet.

_____

5 She sings a song.

_____

6 They eat cookies.

_____

B Complete the chart with the underlined words.

Noun	Verb
baseball	_____
_____	_____
_____	_____

C Look at the underlined words. Write *Noun* or *Verb*.

1 We go to school. _____ Verb

2 We study English. _____

3 We make friends. _____

4 We talk and laugh. _____

5 We join clubs. _____

6 We like school! _____

What actions do you do at school?

A Complete the chart.

uncle ballet chess eat laugh ~~art~~ aunt cousin swim cheer soccer coach

Club	Person	Verb
art		

B Complete the sentences with *There's a* or *There are*.

1 __There's a__ uniform.

2 __________ soccer team.

3 __________ three friends.

4 __________ big beach.

5 __________ two sandcastles.

6 __________ holiday today.

Unit 3 and Me

My learning in this unit

I know about __________________________.

I want to know about __________________________.

What size is a community?

Vocabulary 1

A Look and write the letter.

1 town   <u>a</u>

2 family   ___

3 parade   ___

4 playground   ___

5 song   ___

B Circle the correct option.

1 This is Ms. Gomez. She is a **country** / **teacher**.

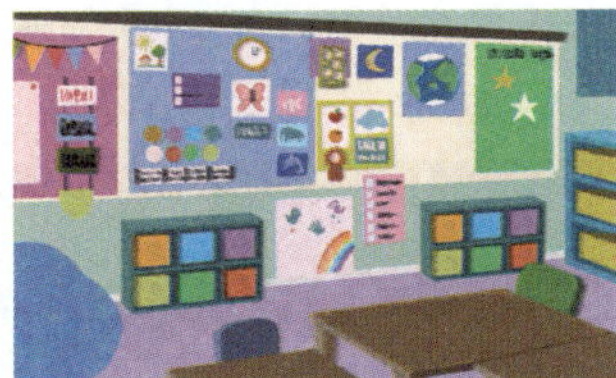

2 This is Ms. Gomez's **classmate** / **classroom** .

3 Sam and Ramon are **classmates** / **families** in Ms. Gomez's class.

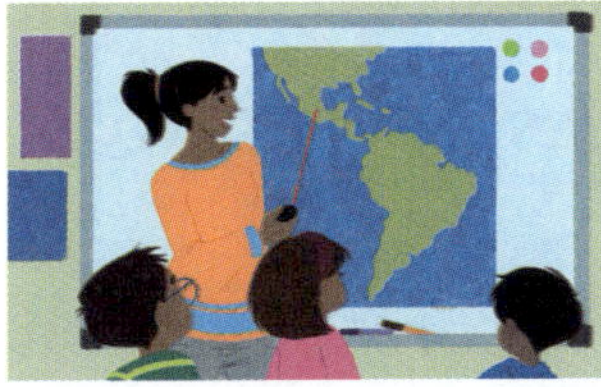

4 Today in class, the students learn about their **country** / **parade** .

5 Later, Ms. Gomez's class has **recess** / **songs** .

6 Sam and Ramon play on the **classroom** / **playground** .

4 Grammar

A Check (✓) Yes or No.

1 The students are under a tree.

Yes ✓ No

2 The classmates are on the playground.

Yes No

3 The teacher is behind the table.

Yes No

4 The boy is next to the bike.

Yes No

5 The book is on the table.

Yes No

6 The pencil is behind the table.

Yes No

B Circle the correct option.

1 The girl isn't **next to** / **on** her table.

2 The pencils are **on** / **next to** the book.

3 The doll is **behind** / **under** the table.

4 The book is **on** / **under** the table.

5 The pencils aren't **under** / **next to** the book.

6 The door is **behind** / **under** the table.

Grammar: Prepositions of Place: *On, Under, Next to, Behind*

C Complete the sentences.

under   behind   next to   on   ~~under~~

1 The duck is ___under___ the chair.
2 The boy is _____________ the tree.
3 The man is _____________ his wife.
4 The bee is _____________ the flower.
5 The ball is _____________ the girl.

D Complete the sentences.

1  The small bird is ___under___ the t<u>ree</u>_____.

2 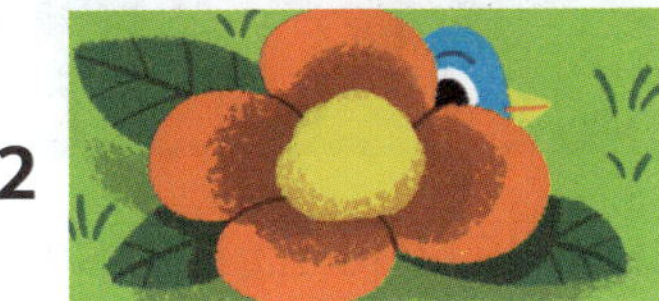 The small bird is _____________ the f_________.

3  The small bird is _____________ a big b_________.

4  The small bird is happy! He is _____________ his friend.

Look. What are you next to?

A Read the story. Which of these are Isabel's communities?
Circle three answers.

family   classmates   animals   toys   team

Isabel's Communities

Hi! I'm Isabel. I belong to some special communities.

This is my family. We're eating breakfast. There are six people in my family.

This is my school's playground. I'm with my teacher and some of my classmates.

I sit next to my friends in music class. We play songs.

This is my soccer team. My coach is behind us. I love soccer!

 Underline these words in the text.

family   playground   teacher   classmates   songs

 Circle the correct option.

1 Who is the subject of the text?

 (Isabel)    the teacher

2 Who does Isabel eat breakfast with?

 Grandpa    the coach

3 Who is on the playground?

 the coach    the teacher

4 Who does Isabel sit next to?

 friends    the team

5 Who is behind the team?

 Isabel    the coach

 Complete the sentences.

six   soccer   playground   ~~family~~   songs

1 Isabel eats breakfast with her _______ family _______.

2 There are _________________ people in Isabel's family.

3 Isabel, her teacher, and her classmates are on the _________________.

4 Isabel and her friends play _________________ in music class.

5 Isabel plays on a _________________ team.

A **Look and write the letter.**

1 bear   _e_
2 deer   __
3 forest   __
4 plant   __
5 rabbit   __
6 squirrel   __

B **Write the letters to complete the words in the sentences.**

1 There is a r _a_ b _b_ _i_ t.

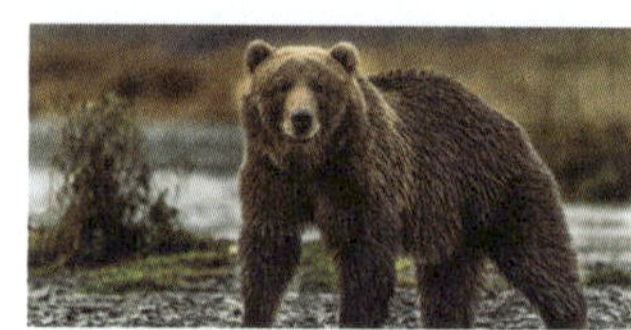

2 This is a brown b __ __ __ .

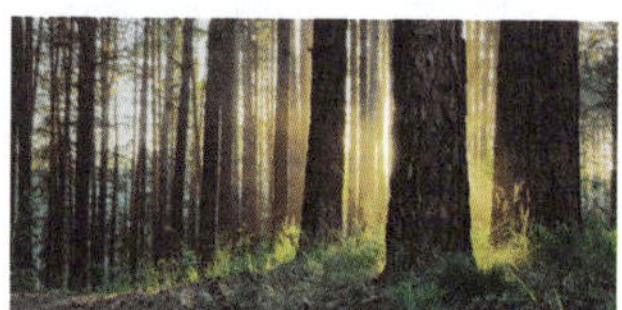

3 It's a big __ __ re __ __ .

4 There is a red s __ __ i __ __ el.

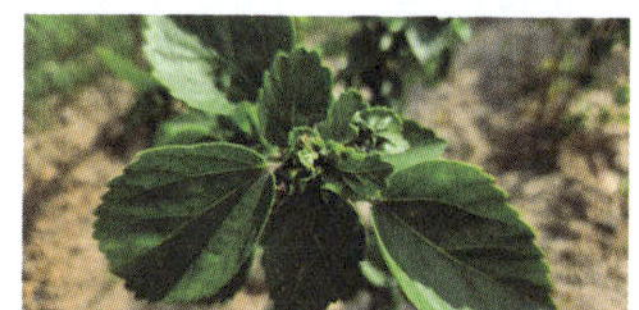

5 It's a green __ __ an __ .

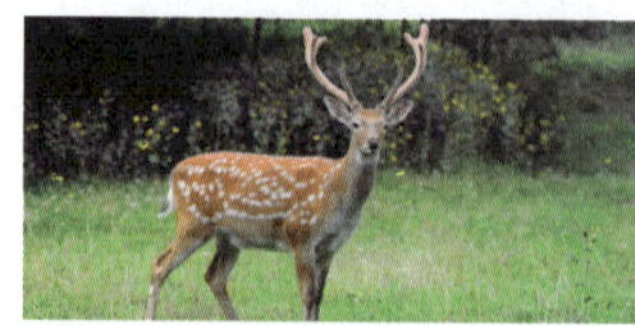

6 This is a big __ __ __ r.

What animals live near your home?

A Match.

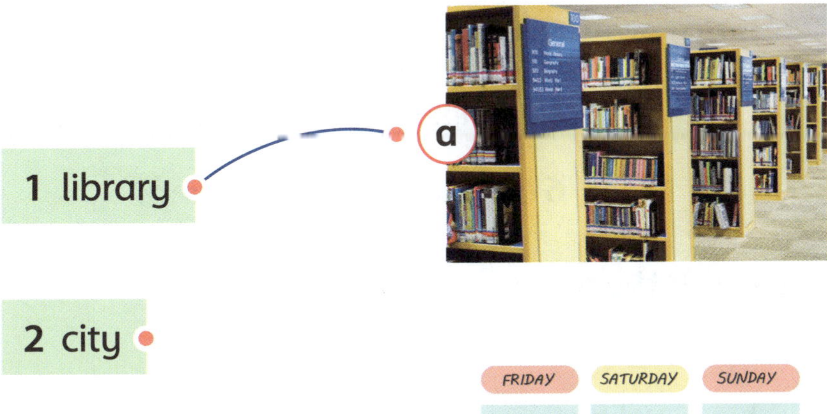

1 library

2 city

3 museum

4 subway

5 village

6 weekend

B Read and complete.

museum   subway   ~~city~~   library   weekend

Amelia lives in a big ¹ _______city_______ . On the
² ___________________ , Amelia and her dad go by
³ ___________________ to the art ⁴ ___________________ .
Then they go to the ⁵ ___________________ to read
books. They have fun!

A **Do the sentences use capital letters and periods? Circle ✓ or ✗.**

1 She lives in a village.   ✓ ✗

2 he lives in a city   ✓ ✗

3 They go to the library.   ✓ ✗

4 The town has a parade   ✓ ✗

5 we like the museum   ✓ ✗

6 I go to the playground.   ✓ ✗

B **Read and complete. Use capital letters.**

1 _____This_____ (this) is Kenji.

2 ___________ (he) lives in a town.

3 ___________ (his) favorite place is the library. **4** ___________ (kenji) goes there on the weekends with his mom.

5 ___________ (they) read books.

C **Correct the sentences using capital letters and periods.**

1 the girl is in a classroom

____

____

2 she's next to the desk

____

____

3 the books are on the desk

____

____

A Cross out (X) the one that doesn't belong.

1 ~~bear~~   city   village

2 library   museum   song

3 deer   playground   squirrel

4 classmate   teacher   weekend

B Complete the sentences.

plant   family   ~~parade~~

~~on~~   behind   next to   under

1 The _____parade_____ is _____on_____ the street.

2 The library is _____________ the museum.

3 The library is _____________ the _____________ .

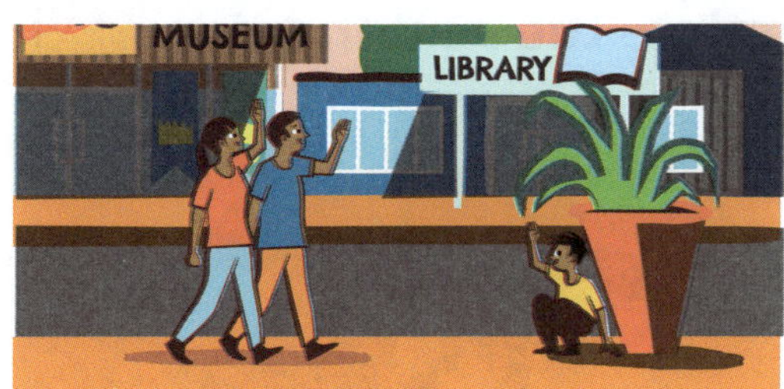

4 The boy is _____________ the _____________ .

Unit 4 and Me

My learning in this unit

I know about ____ .

I want to know about _______________________________________ .

5 Why do we need communities?

A Look and write the letter.

1 baby   c
2 drink   __
3 lion   __
4 mother   __
5 water   __

B Complete the sentences.

herd   find   ~~helps~~   safe   leader

1 The mother _____ helps _____ her baby eat.

2 The lions walk to _____________ water.

3 The _____________ walks behind the _____________.

4 The elephants keep the babies _____________.

A **Match the questions to the answers.**

1 Where is the baby elephant?   **a** It is behind the tree.

2 Where is the rabbit?   **b** It is on the plant.

3 Where is the spider?   **c** It's behind the plant.

4 Where's the lion?   **d** It's under the tree.

5 Where's the squirrel?   **e** It's next to the water.

B **Look and write the letters to answer the questions.**

1 Where are the rabbits?   _d_   **a** They are next to the flowers.

2 Where are the bears?   ___   **b** They are on the flowers.

3 Where are the bees?   ___   **c** They're under the tree.

4 Where are the deer?   ___   **d** They're behind the plant.

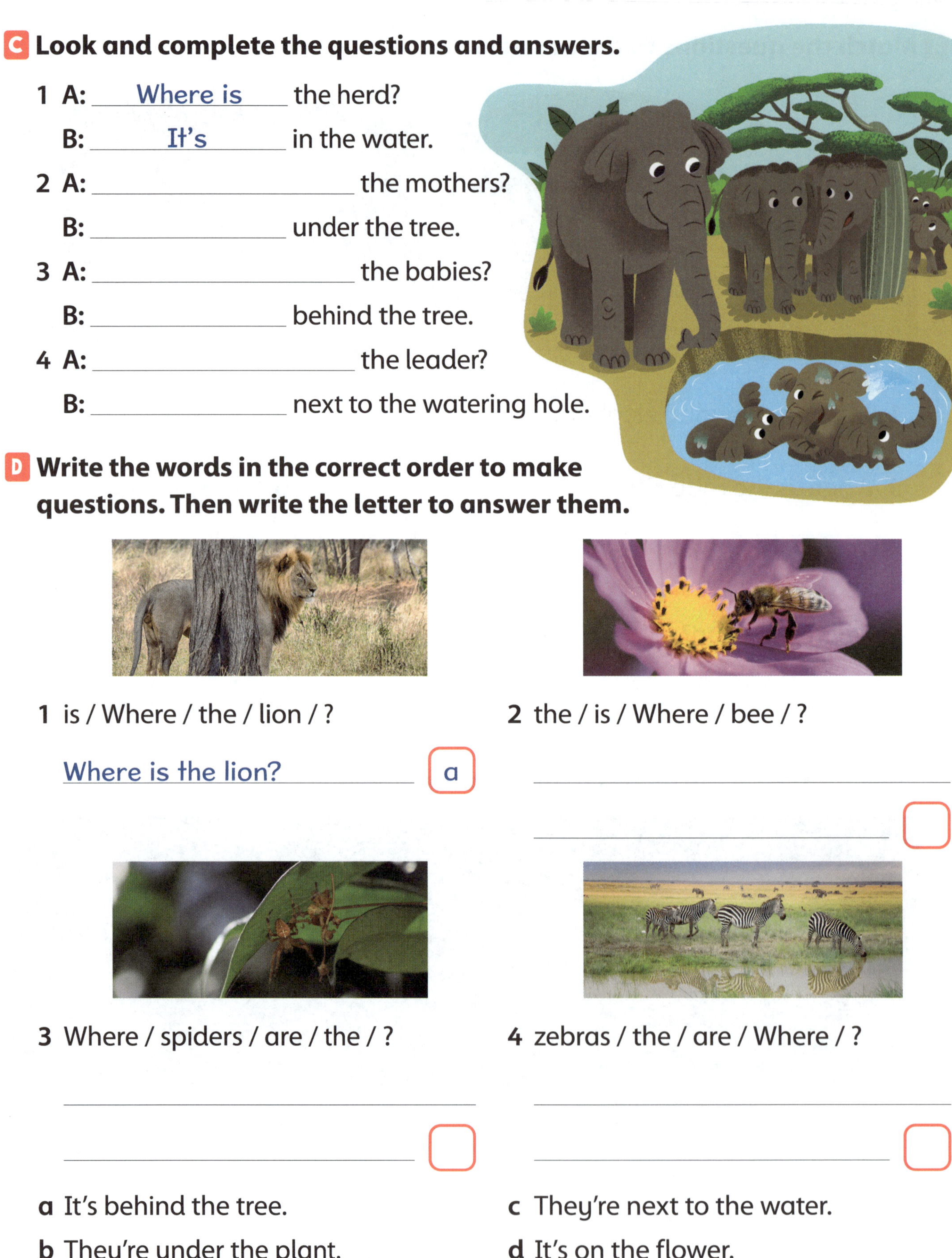

D Write the words in the correct order to make questions. Then write the letter to answer them.

1 is / Where / the / lion / ?

<u>Where is the lion?</u>   [a]

2 the / is / Where / bee / ?

3 Where / spiders / are / the / ?

4 zebras / the / are / Where / ?

a It's behind the tree.

b They're under the plant.

c They're next to the water.

d It's on the flower.

A **Read the magazine article. What is the subject of the text? Circle.**

babies   lions   water

Lion Communities

Lions are special animals. They live in many countries in Africa. They live in a community called a pride.

Where are the baby lions? They're with their mothers. Mother lions work together to help the babies.

Baby lions drink milk. Big lions drink water. They can also get water from plants, like this melon.

Lions also work together to find food. They're an animal team!

B **Underline these words in the text.**

mothers   help   drink   water   find

C **Circle _True_ or _False_.**

1 Lions live in Africa.	(True)	False
2 A community of lions is called a herd.	True	False
3 Mother lions work together.	True	False
4 Big lions drink milk.	True	False
5 Lions can get water from plants.	True	False

D **Match the questions to the answers.**

1 What is a community of lions called?   **a** water

2 What do mother lions do together?   **b** a pride

3 What do baby lions drink?   **c** help the babies

4 What do big lions drink?   **d** food

5 What do lions work together to find?   **e** milk

A **Look and write the letter.**

1 coral reef   <u>e</u>
2 shark   __
3 ocean   __
4 seagrass   __
5 turtle   __
6 crab   __

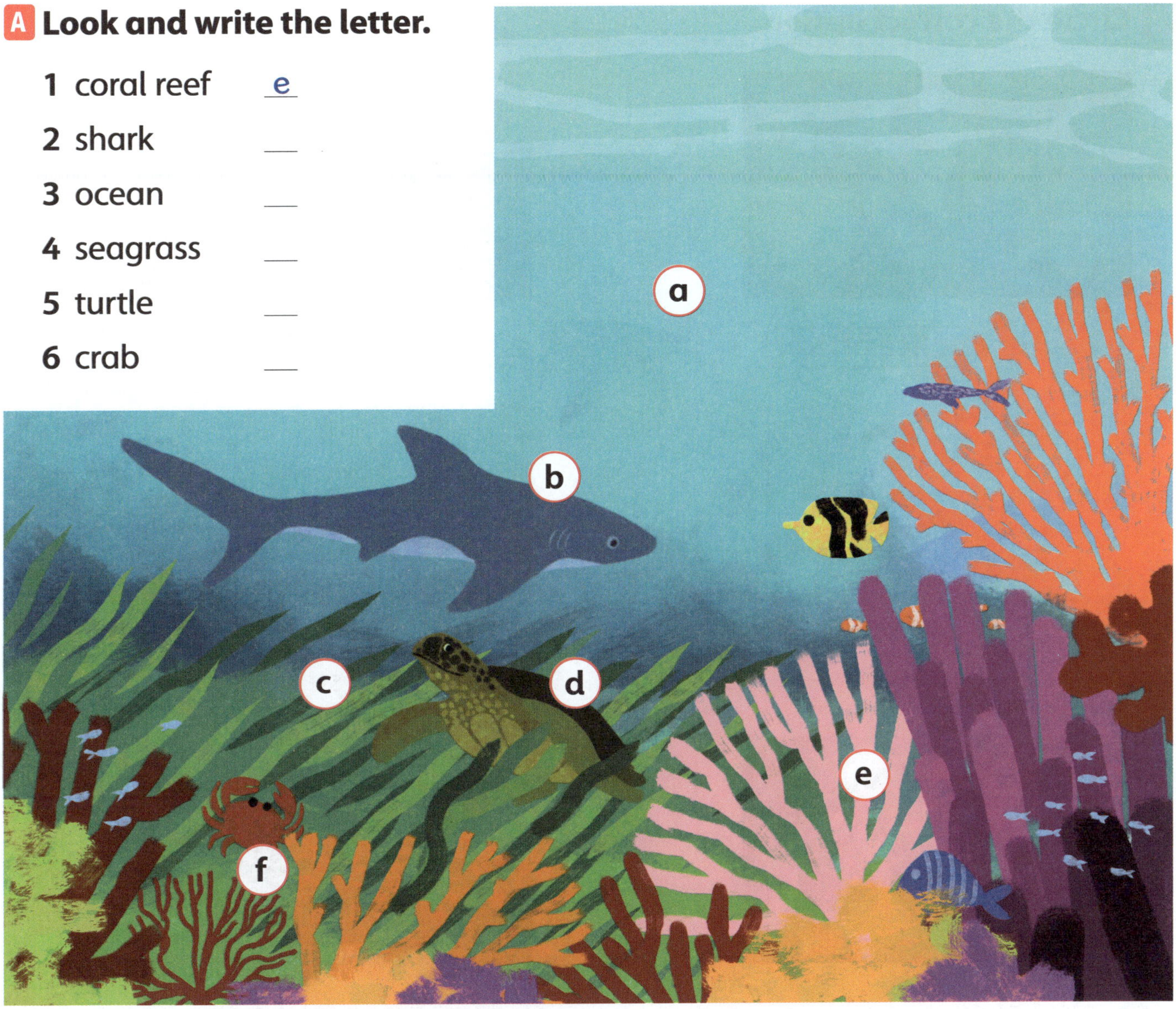

B **Complete the words in the sentences.**

1 The <u>shark</u> is swimming.
2 The c<u>   </u> is walking on the sand.
3 The c<u>   </u> r<u>   </u> has many colors.
4 There's a t<u>   </u> in the s<u>   </u>.
5 These animals live in a community in the o<u>   </u>.

What is your favorite ocean animal?

A Circle the correct option.

1 doctor / **police officer**

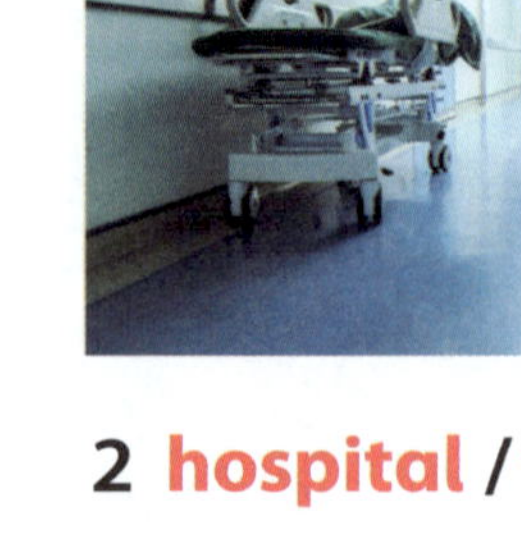

2 hospital / work

3 doctor / mail carrier

4 hospital / supermarket

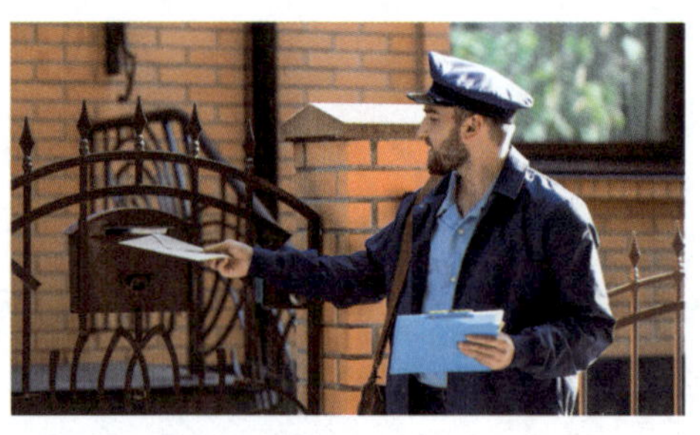

5 mail carrier / police officer

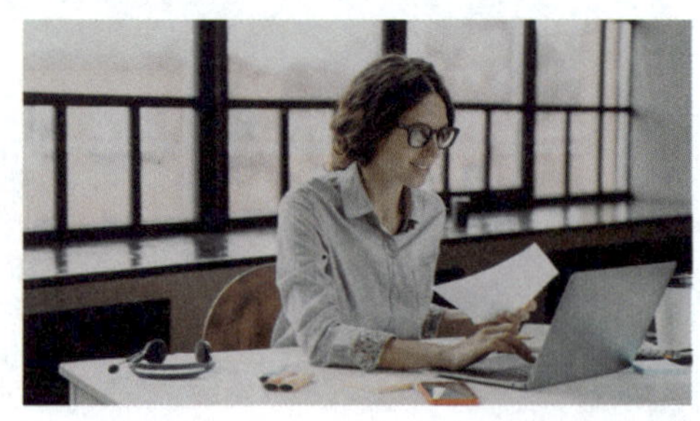

6 supermarket / work

B Complete the sentences.

mail carriers   police officers   doctors   hospital   supermarket   ~~work~~

1 People ________ work ________ in many places in our community.

2 Nurses work with ________________ to keep us healthy.

3 ________________ keep us safe in our towns and cities.

4 ________________ bring mail to our homes.

5 Doctors and nurses work in the ________________.

6 We go to the ________________ when we want to get food.

A Write the adjectives.

1 That's a beautiful ocean. __beautiful__

2 It's a funny fish. ______________

3 The big turtle swims in the sea. ______________

4 This is a red crab. ______________

5 She likes the friendly rabbit. ______________

6 The elephant is a good leader. ______________

B Look at the underlined words. Write *N* for noun or *A* for adjective.

1 Dolphins are <u>special</u> animals.   A

2 They are <u>good</u> swimmers.   __

3 They live in big <u>communities</u> called pods.   __

4 Baby dolphins eat <u>small</u> fish.   __

5 Mother dolphins swim next to their small <u>babies</u>.   __

C Read and write the adjectives.

Alice has a kind doctor. Dr. McCarthy wears a white shirt. She has blond hair. She works in a big hospital. Alice likes Dr. McCarthy!

1 ______________

2 ______________

3 ______________

4 ______________

Describe a friend. Use adjectives.

A Write the words in the correct groups.

herd   shark   mail carrier   find   ~~supermarket~~

1 school, hospital, _supermarket_

2 community, family, ______________

3 doctor, police officer, ______________

4 help, work, ______________

5 turtle, crab, ______________

B Complete the questions and answers.

1 A: Where _____ are _____ the lions?

  B: They're next to the _____ water _____.

2 A: Where ______________ the ______________?

  B: It's on the flower.

3 A: Where ______________ the turtles?

  B: They're in the ______________.

4 A: ______________ the ______________?

  B: She's at our home.

5 A: ______________ the mother?

  B: She's in the ______________.

6 A: ______________ the doctor?

  B: He's in the ______________.

Unit 5 and Me

My learning in this unit   

I know about ____.

I want to know about ____.

6 How can communities make our lives better?

A Look and write the letter.

1 make a snowman   <u>d</u>

2 neighborhood   ___

3 nervous   ___

4 online   ___

5 share   ___

B Read and complete.

gloves   cold   <u>outside</u>   weather   lonely

Nicolas is playing ¹ _____<u>outside</u>_____ today.
He wears a coat and hat because the
² ________________ is very ³ ________________ .
He also wears ⁴ ________________ on his hands.
Nicolas feels ⁵ ________________ because his
friends aren't in the neighborhood today.

A Match.

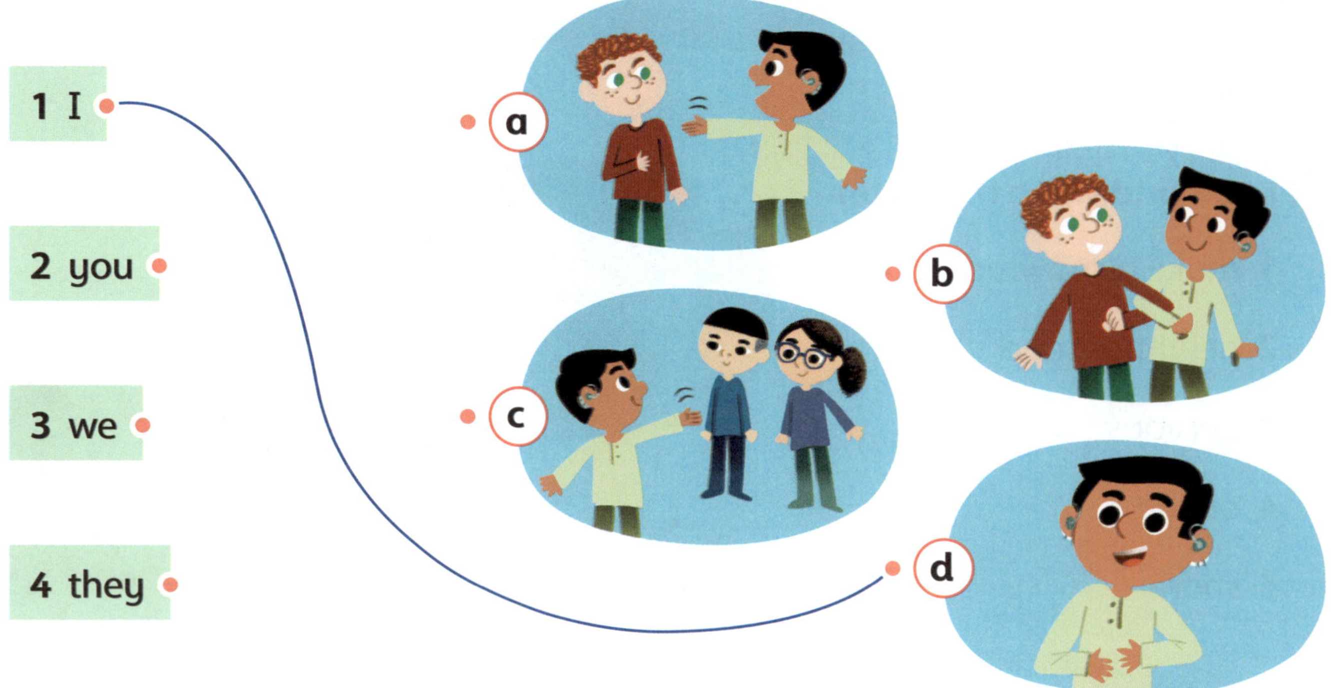

1 I

2 you

3 we

4 they

a

b

c

d

B Circle the correct option.

1 (**I**) / **They** make a snowman.

2 **We** / **You** play outside.

3 **They** / **You** wear gloves.

4 **We** / **They** eat pizza.

5 **They** / **I** see rabbits!

6 **I** / **We** have fun!

feel   make   share   play

1 You _______ feel _______ lonely at a new school.

2 We _______________ soccer with our friends outside.

3 They _______________ a snowman after school.

4 I _______________ my dolls with my friends.

D **Write the words in the correct order to make sentences.**
Then write the letter of the picture.

1 live / in / a / neighborhood / I / big / .

I live in a big neighborhood. _______________ **d**

2 We / playing / like / outside / .

____

3 under / tree / the / read / They / .

____

4 to / talk / You / your / friends online / .

____

A New Friend for Yasmin

Yasmin likes her neighborhood. She has good friends here. They play outside.

Today, Yasmin sees a new girl. She looks nervous and lonely.

Yasmin is kind. She wants to help.

The children play with Jana. They make friends. They have fun together.

Jana isn't lonely now. She has new friends and a new community.

 Underline these words in the text.

neighborhood   outside   nervous   lonely   share

 Match.

| 1 beginning | 2 middle | 3 end |

a

b

c

 Circle _True_ or _False_.

1	Yasmin likes her neighborhood.	**True**	False
2	Yasmin is lonely.	True	False
3	Jana is new in the neighborhood.	True	False
4	Yasmin and her friends are kind.	True	False
5	Yasmin doesn't share toys.	True	False
6	Jana makes new friends.	True	False

What can you share with friends?

A **Look and write the word.**

fun   comic book   take photos   ~~upload~~   story   website

1 _____upload_____

2 __________

3 __________

4 __________

5 __________

6 __________

B **Circle the correct option.**

1 Philippe and Dara **take photos** / **upload** of nature.

2 They have **comic book** / **fun** together outside.

3 Later, they **story** / **upload** their photos to a website.

4 Jen goes online to a **comic book** / **website** after school.

5 She reads a funny **story** / **upload**.

 **What do you do for fun?**

A **Look and write the letter.**

1 carry   _e_
2 wash the car   __
3 greet   __
4 neighbor   __
5 cookies   __
6 snacks   __

B **Complete the sentences.**

1 Carly goes to see her _neighbor_ .
2 Ms. Santos says hello to g____________ Carly.
3 Carly brings s____________ for Ms. Santos to eat.
4 Ms. Santos loves c____________ !
5 Then Carly helps her father w____________ the c____________ .

A Complete the chart.

> What do you like?   I like cookies.   I'm Jen.
> Where's your book?   It's on the desk.   Who are you?

Questions	Sentences
What do you like?	

B Are the question marks and periods correct? Check (✓) or cross (✗).

1 What's Yasmin's favorite sport?   ✓

2 Yasmin loves soccer?   ___

3 She plays with her friends.   ___

4 Where does Yasmin play.   ___

5 Yasmin plays at school.   ___

C Write a question mark or a period.

1 **Yildiz:** What's your favorite snack **?**
   Drew: I like apples ___

2 **Aiko:** Where are the crabs ___
   Thabo: They're in the ocean ___

3 **Abi:** I have new gloves ___
   Bill: What color are your gloves ___

A **Cross out (X) the one that doesn't belong.**

1 cookie	~~greet~~	snack
2 neighbor	upload	website
3 carry	comic book	story
4 cold	weather	wash the car
5 lonely	neighborhood	nervous

B **Complete the sentences. Use one word from each box.**

~~I~~   They   We   You   share   wash   take   ~~carry~~

1 _____I carry_____ books to my kitchen.

2 _________________ our comic books.

3 _________________ photos of the deer.

4 _________________ the car.

Unit 6 and Me

My learning in this unit         

I know about ____.

I want to know about ____.

7 How do we celebrate our culture?

A Look and write the word.

boots   jeans   long   belt   shirt   ~~hat~~

1 _____hat_____
2 _______________
3 _______________
4 _______________
5 _______________
6 _______________

B Complete the sentences.

colorful   wear   ~~beautiful~~   clothes

1 Traditional clothes are _____beautiful_____ .

2 She wants to _______________ the pink shirt.

3 She has a _______________ hat.

4 He carries a lot of _______________ .

7 Grammar

A **Match.**

1 he   2 it   3 she

B **Circle the correct option.**

1 She **wear** / **wears** a hat at sports games.

2 She **live** / **lives** in Canada.

3 She **loves** / **love** sports.

4 He **like** / **likes** wearing jeans.

5 He **read** / **reads** comic books every Saturday.

6 He has a cat. It **drinks** / **drink** milk.

 Write the words in the correct order to make sentences.

1 at home / jeans / He / wears / .

He wears jeans at home.

2 My sister / South Korea / lives / in / .

____

3 David / colorful / likes / clothes / .

____

4 shirt / The / good / feels / .

____

D **Complete the sentences. Use the correct form of a verb from the box.**

> wear   greet   ~~live~~   upload   like   share

1 He _____lives_____ with his grandma and grandpa.

2 She _______________ a skirt at school.

3 He _______________ playing soccer with friends.

4 My neighbor _______________ me every morning.

5 She _______________ books at the book club.

6 The teacher _______________ photos every Friday.

A Read the article. Where do Alba and James live?

Clothes that Celebrate Culture

My name is Alba. I live in Panama. Sometimes I wear a *pollera*. My sister wears a pollera, too. Polleras are traditional clothes in Panama. A pollera is a shirt and a long skirt. Many polleras are white, but some are colorful. Polleras usually have pictures of animals or flowers. These clothes are important in my community in Panama. Polleras are beautiful!

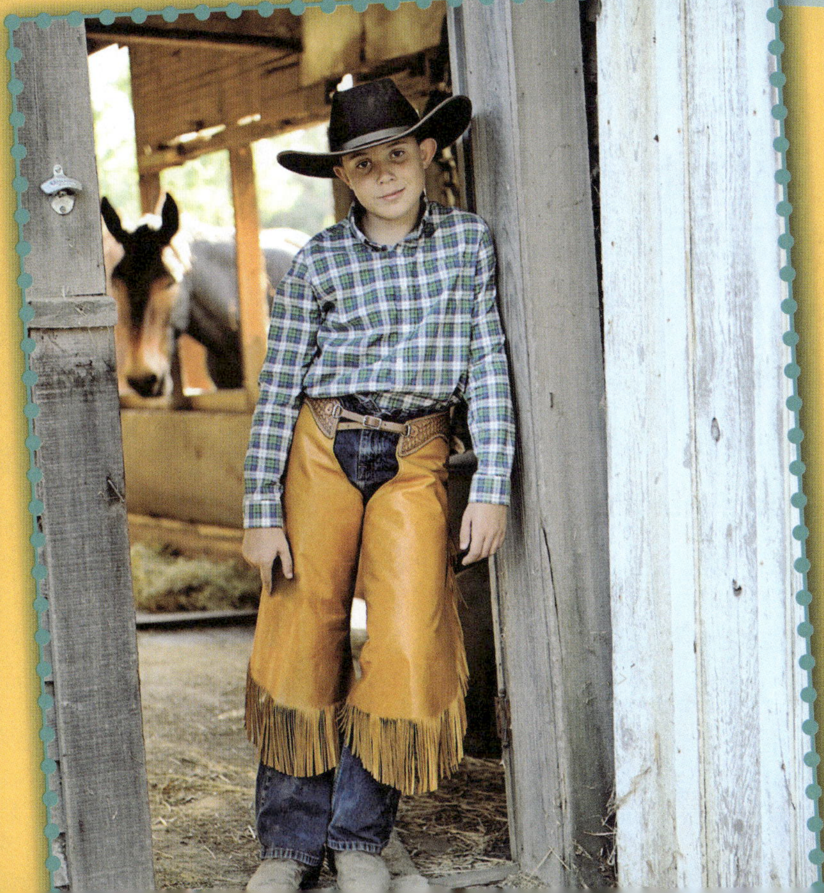

Hi! My name is James. I live in Texas, in the United States. There are many big farms in Texas. My family works on a farm. Sometimes I help them. I wear clothes that are good for farm work. I usually wear jeans, boots, and a hat. These clothes keep me safe from the sun and animals. I feel like a part of the community in Texas when I wear these traditional clothes.

shirt   long   skirt   jeans   boots   hat

C Categorize. Complete the chart.

flowers   hat   ~~colorful~~   jeans   skirt   boots

Traditional Clothes in ...

Panama	Texas

colorful	

D Circle the correct option.

1 Polleras are traditional clothes in **Panama** / **Texas** .

2 A pollera has a skirt and a **hat** / **shirt** .

3 Alba thinks polleras are **beautiful** / **long** .

4 James wears clothes to work **in a garden** / **on a farm** .

5 His clothes keep him safe from the **community** / **sun** .

What are traditional clothes in your culture?

Vocabulary 2

A Look and write the word.

give   envelope   ~~New Year~~   grapes   fireworks   throw

1 __New Year__

2 __________

3 __________

4 __________

5 __________

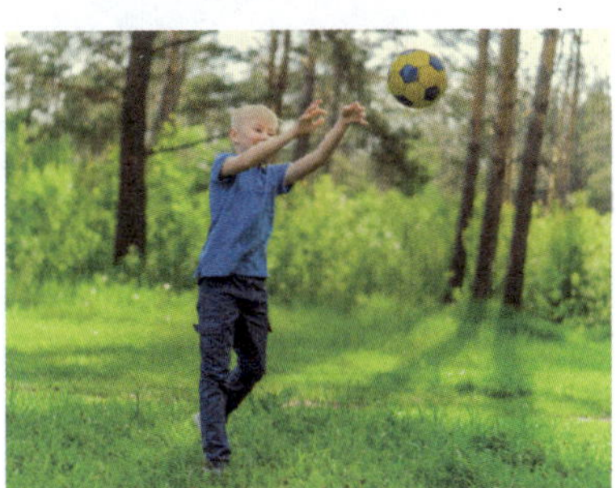

6 __________

B Match to make sentences.

1 They eat …

2 We watch …

3 I celebrate …

4 She throws …

5 Parents give …

a fireworks.

b water on friends.

c grapes to celebrate.

d New Year with my friends.

e envelopes to children.

How do you celebrate the New Year?

Vocabulary 3

A Check (✓) the correct option.

1 ☑ loud ☐ soft

2 ☐ history ☐ music

3 ☐ history ☐ musician

4 ☐ instruments ☐ musician

5 ☐ instruments ☐ soft

6 ☐ history ☐ loud

B Circle the correct option.

1 The students aren't in (history)/ **soft** class.

2 They are in **music** / **musician** class.

3 They play their **instruments** / **musicians** .

4 The music is **loud** / **instrument** .

A **Match the opposites.**

1 sad

2 same

3 calm

4 black

a white

b nervous

c different

d happy

B **Circle the opposite.**

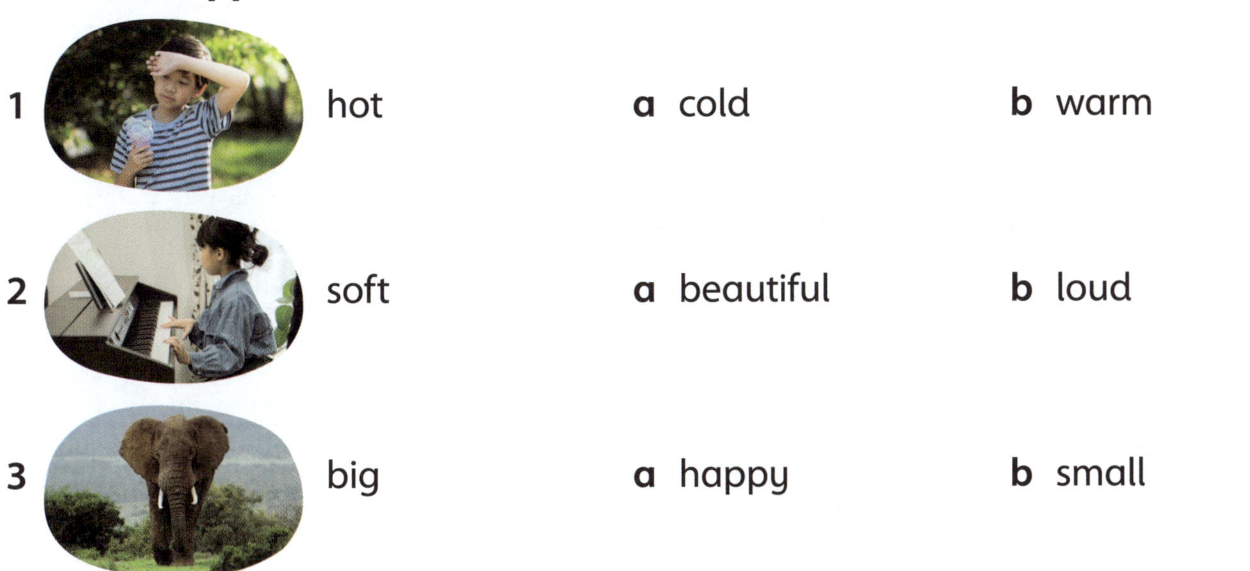

1 hot   **a** cold   **b** warm

2 soft   **a** beautiful   **b** loud

3 big   **a** happy   **b** small

A **Write the words in the correct groups.**

colorful ~~hat~~ wear fireworks

1 belt, boots, _____hat_____

2 beautiful, soft, _____________

3 give, throw, _____________

4 New Year, grapes, _____________

B **Are the sentences correct? Check (✓) or cross (✗).**
Correct the sentences with a cross.

1 ✗ He wear boots every day.

He **wears** boots every day.

____

2 ☐ She ride a bike to school.

____

____

3 ☐ The rabbit eats plants.

____

____

4 ☐ He swim every weekend.

____

____

Unit 7 and Me

My learning in this unit

I know about _____________________________ .

I want to know about _____________________________ .

8 Where do we experience culture?

A Look and circle the correct option.

1 sandwich / **vegetables**
2 chicken / chili peppers
3 sandwich / yogurt
4 bottle / yogurt

5 exciting / salad
6 bottle / chicken
7 chili peppers / salad

B Match.

1 This sandwich is delicious.

2 We're watching fireworks – it's exciting!

3 I'm a vegetarian.

a

b

c

A Match the opposites.

1 I eat meat.

2 He makes cookies.

3 She drinks water.

4 We eat chili peppers.

5 It likes chicken.

6 They wear hats.

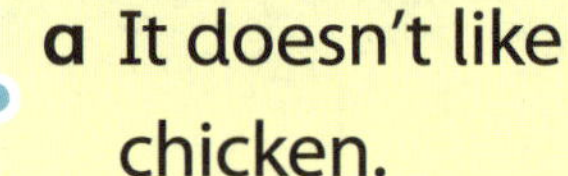

a It doesn't like chicken.

b They don't wear hats.

c She doesn't drink water.

d He doesn't make cookies.

e I don't eat meat.

f We don't eat chili peppers.

B Look at the underlined words. Check (✓) the correct option.

1 I <u>do not</u> make chicken sandwiches. ☐ doesn't ☐ don't

2 She <u>does not</u> make her lunch. ☐ doesn't ☐ don't

3 It <u>does not</u> eat food. ☐ doesn't ☐ don't

4 We <u>do not</u> like yogurt. ☐ doesn't ☐ don't

5 They <u>do not</u> have any bottles. ☐ doesn't ☐ don't

What is a food you don't like?

 Write the words in the correct order to make sentences.

1 lunch / make / I / do / not / .

   I do not make lunch.

2 She / not / chicken / does / eat / .

   ____

3 doesn't / salad / like / He / .

   ____

4 have / We / sandwiches / don't / .

   ____

5 eat / chili peppers / don't / They / .

   ____

D **Write the negative sentences.**

1 Eloise likes yogurt.

   Eloise doesn't like yogurt.

2 The tree has apples.

   ____

3 Dineo eats meat.

   ____

4 They make breakfast.

   ____

 Read the story. What day is it in Class 1B?

Our Favorite Foods

Mrs. Ellis and Class 1B want to learn more about food. They have a Favorite Food Day today! Each classmate has a special food from home. They tell the class about their foods.

B **Underline these words in the text.**

sandwich   delicious   yogurt   chicken

C **Circle the words in the story. How many times do you see each word?**

delicious __   favorite __   food/foods __

D **Circle the correct option.**

1 Class 1B wants to learn more about **food** / **sandwiches** .

2 **Mateo** / **Yan** has a food with eggs.

3 Larisa's food has **chicken** / **yogurt** .

4 Larisa **likes** / **doesn't like** spicy foods.

5 Yan **has** / **doesn't have** his favorite food.

6 Yan and his **dad** / **mom** make food together every week.

Which food from the story do you want to eat?

A **Look and write the letter.**

1 café   b
2 art museum   __
3 sidewalk   __
4 plate   __

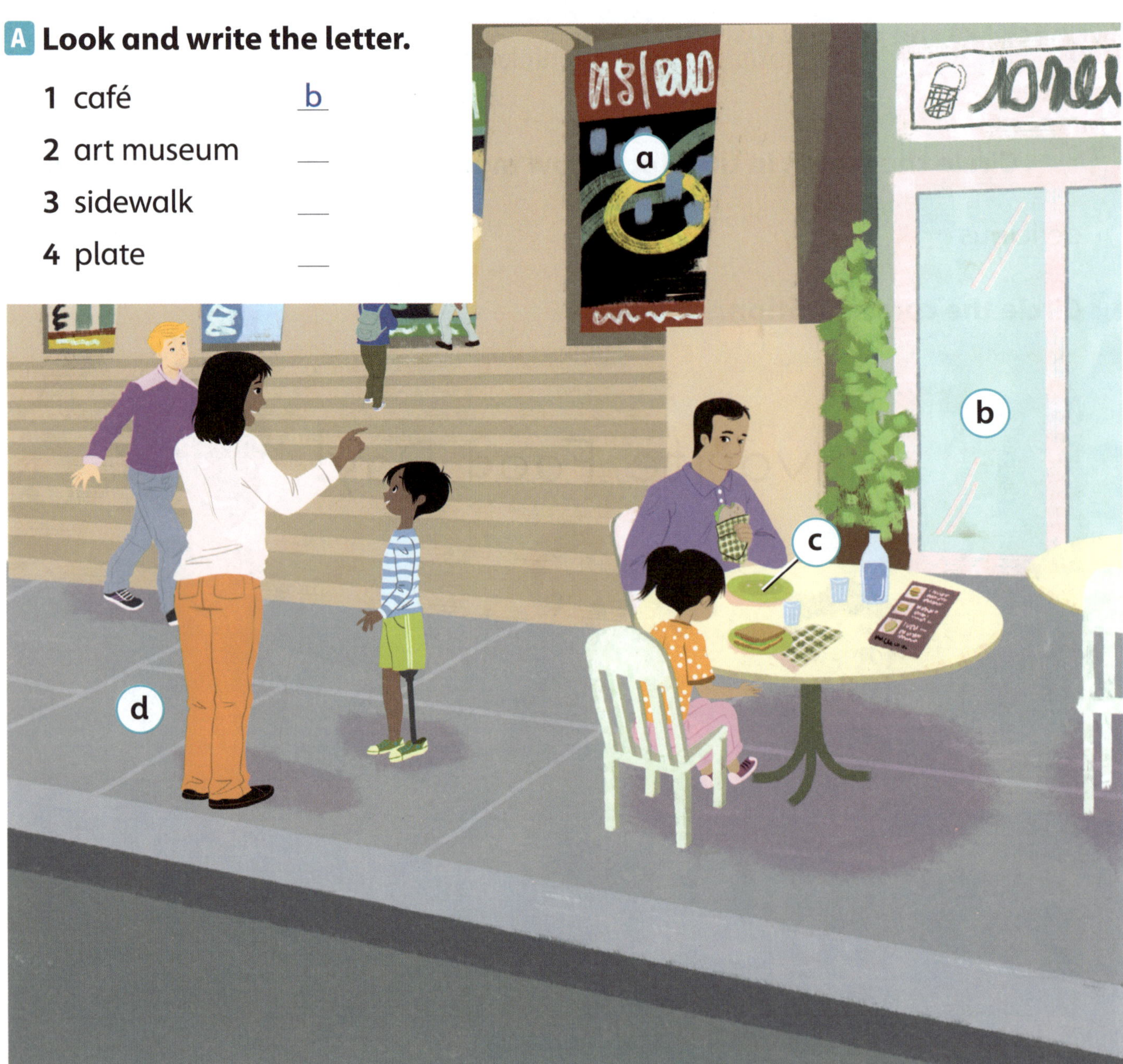

B **Complete the sentences.**

café   buildings   sidewalk   interesting

1 This city has many big ____buildings____ .
2 Walk on the ______________ to be safe.
3 We can have lunch in this ______________ .
4 Then, we can go to the art museum. It's very ______________ .

A Check (✓) the correct option.

1 ✓ alphabet
   ☐ words

2 ☐ left
   ☐ right

3 ☐ letter
   ☐ thousand

4 ☐ words
   ☐ letter

5 ☐ right
   ☐ words

6 ☐ left
   ☐ thousand

B Complete the sentences.   left   letter   ~~word~~   right

1 The girl writes a ______word______ .

2 The boy writes a ________________ .

3 She writes with her ________________ hand.

4 He writes with his ________________ hand.

A Circle the exclamation points.

B Write an exclamation point, a question mark, or a period.

1 I have a sandwich_.

2 This yogurt is delicious__

3 My friend is a vegetarian__

4 Where is the art museum__

5 We love chili peppers__

6 What foods do you like__

C Complete the sentences and write an exclamation point.

1 I love ________________________ __

2 This ____________________ is delicious__

A Write *F* for food or *P* for place.

1 chili pepper — F
2 art museum — ___
3 café — ___
4 vegetables — ___

5 yogurt — ___
6 salad — ___
7 sidewalk — ___
8 sandwich — ___

B Complete the sentences.

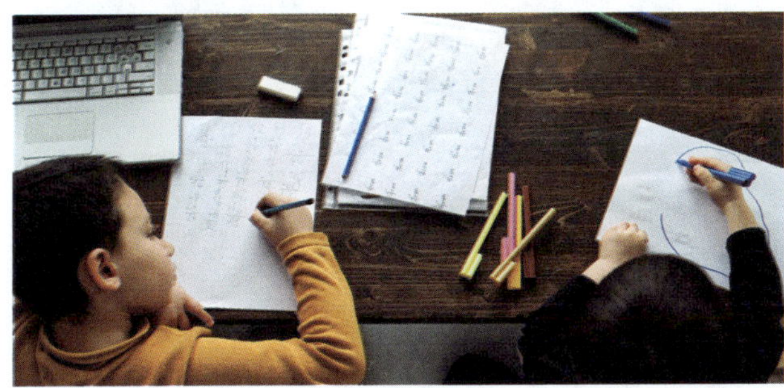

1 They ___don't write___ with their left hands. (not write)

2 He _________________ chicken. (not eat)

3 She _________________ Spanish. (not speak)

4 The class _________________ a thousand students. (not have)

Unit 8 and Me

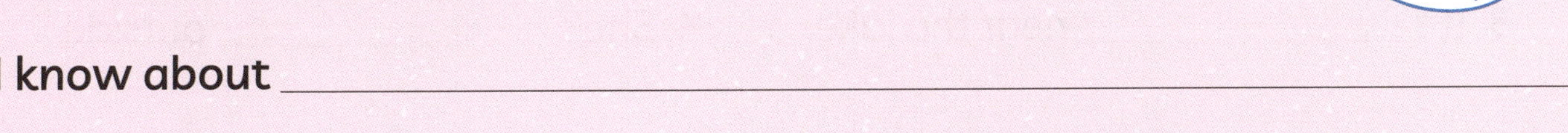

My learning in this unit

I know about ____ .

I want to know about _________________________________ .

9 Why is learning about other cultures important?

A Look and write the letter.

1 boat   <u>d</u>
2 climb   ___
3 horse   ___
4 mountain   ___
5 meat   ___
6 seafood   ___
7 thirsty   ___
8 visit   ___

B Complete the sentences with *warm* or *cool*.

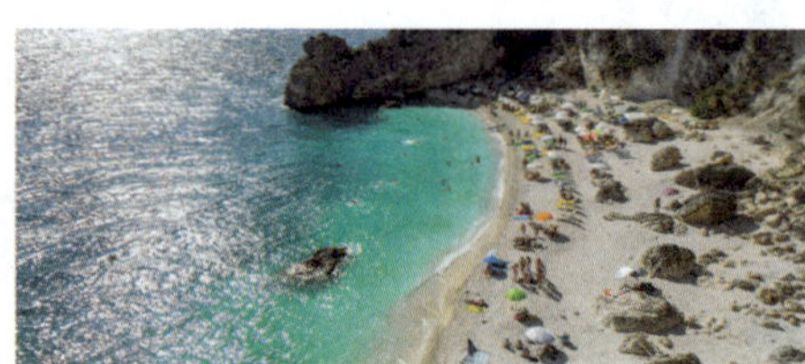

1 It's _____warm_____ at the beach today.

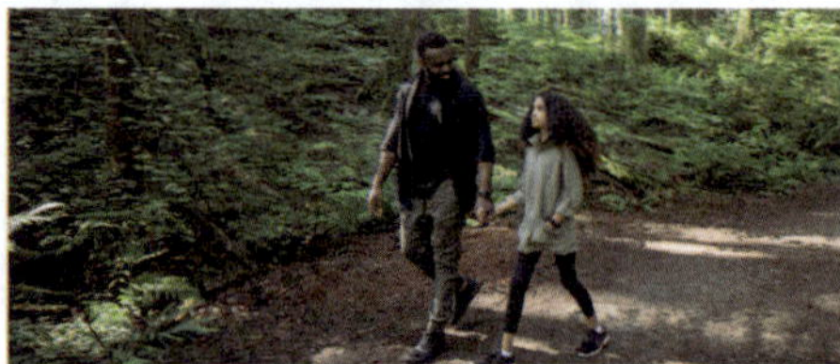

2 It's _____________ in the forest today.

3 It's _____________ near the lake.

4 She's _____________ outside.

What do you wear when it's cool?

A **Check (✓) the correct answer.**

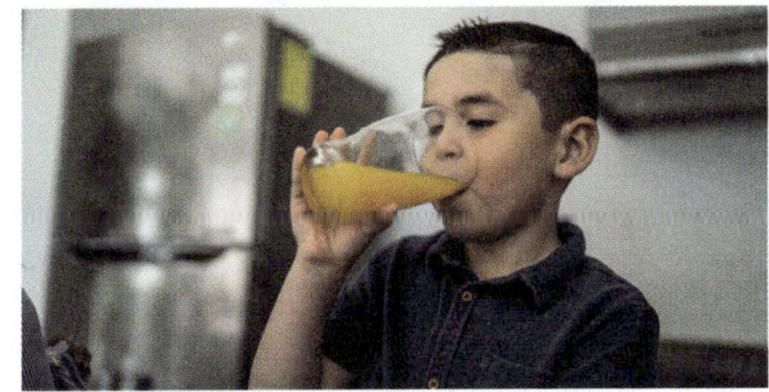

1 Do you drink juice?

- ✓ Yes, I do.
- ☐ No, I don't.

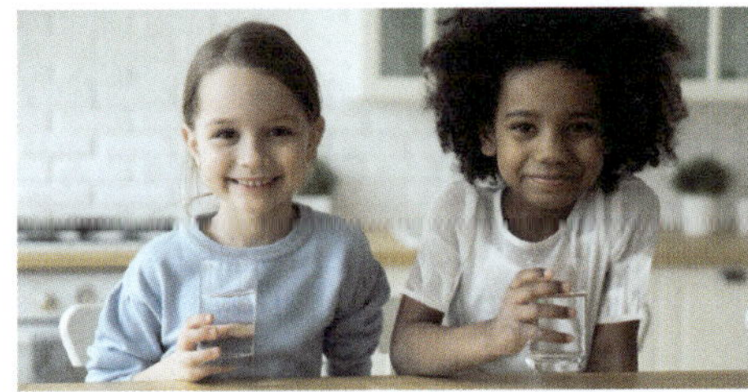

2 Do we have water?

- ☐ Yes, we do.
- ☐ No, we don't.

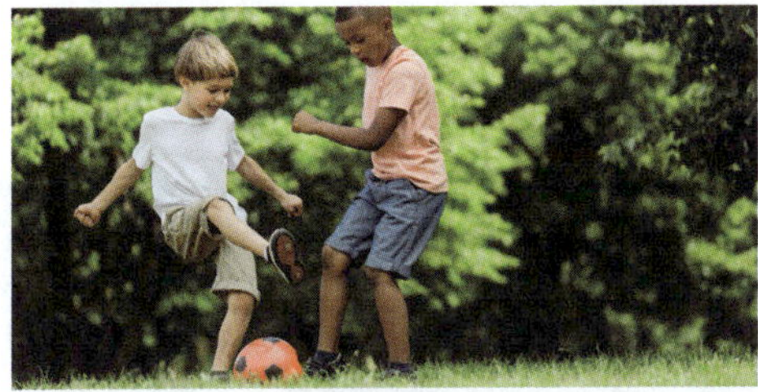

3 Do they have warm clothes?

- ☐ Yes, they do.
- ☐ No, they don't.

4 Do you eat chili peppers?

- ☐ Yes, I do.
- ☐ No, I don't.

B **Complete the answers.**

1 Do you visit your cousins?

Yes, I _______ do _______ .

2 Do you play games together?

Yes, we _______________ .

3 Do they live in a village?

No, they _______________ .

4 Do they live in a city?

Yes, they _______________ .

5 Do you live near them?

No, I _______________ .

 Write the words in the correct order to make questions.

1 sit there / I / Do / ?

<u>Do I sit there?</u>

2 drink milk / Do / you / ?

____

3 we / have vegetables / Do / ?

____

4 they / Do / like seafood / ?

____

D **Complete the questions and write the answers.**

1 A: <u>   Do you   </u> like seafood?

B: <u>Yes, I do.</u>

2 A: ________________ have horses?

B: ________________________________

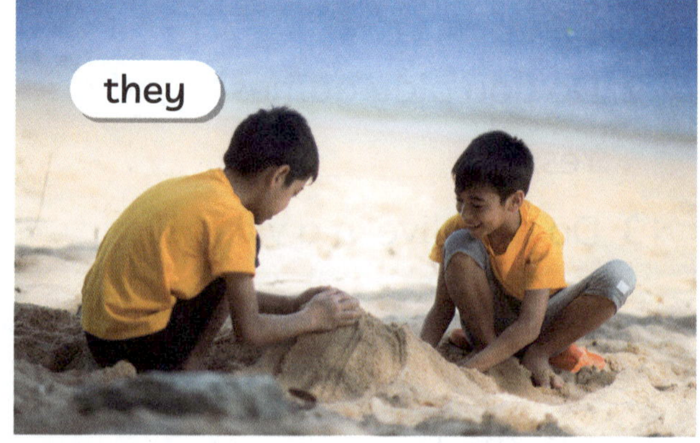

3 A: ________________ travel by boat?

B: ________________________________

4 A: ______________ climb mountains?

B: ________________________________

A **Read the story. Who does Roberto meet?**

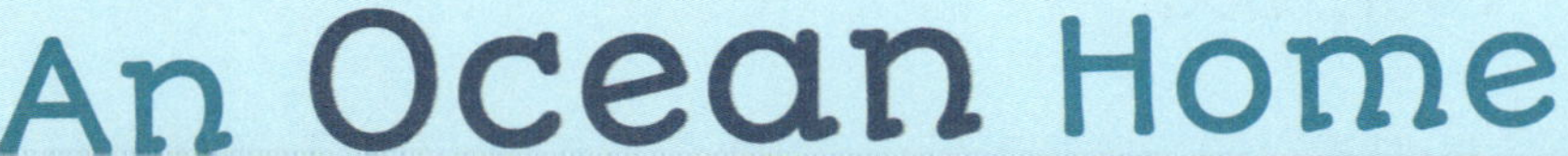

An Ocean Home

Roberto lives in a village near the ocean.
The weather is warm today, so Roberto is
sitting on the beach to eat his lunch.
Roberto sees two people riding
horses on the beach.

 Underline these words in the text.

warm   horses   seafood   cool   boat

 Who are the main characters in the story? Check (✓).

☐ Lina and Aunt Marian

☐ the horses

☐ Roberto and Lina

☐ Roberto's mom

 Circle *True* or *False*.

1 The weather is warm. (True)   False
2 Roberto lives in a village in the mountains. True   False
3 Lina is visiting her grandma. True   False
4 Lina likes seafood. True   False
5 Roberto gives Lina fish and water. True   False
6 Lina wants to go in the boat. True   False

What do you eat or drink when it's warm?

A **Circle the correct option.**

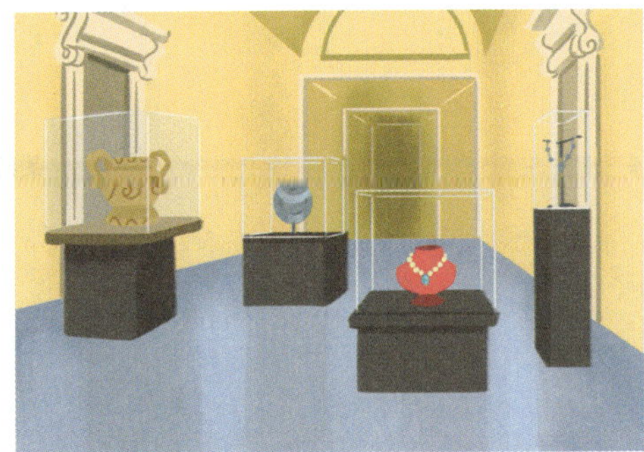

1 board game /(exhibit)

2 model / movie

3 free time / look after

4 exhibit / movie

5 board game / model

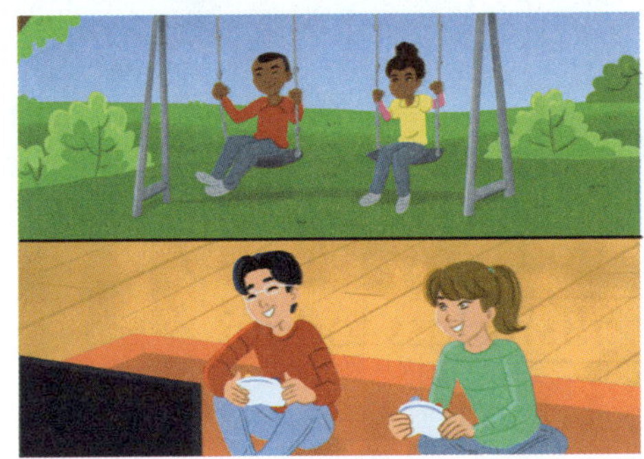

6 free time / look after

B **Write the letters to complete the words in the dialogue.**

Abby: Do you want to play a [1] b o a r d g a m e ?

Zehra: No, I don't. I want to see the horse [2] e __ h __ __ i __ at the museum.

Abby: The museum isn't open. Let's watch a [3] __ o __ __ e .

Zehra: OK. Let's make a [4] m __ __ __ __ l car first.

Abby: Good idea. But first we have to [5] l o __ __ a __ __ e __ the cat.

A **Read and complete.**

> Science   homework   ~~English~~   Video chat

Wednesday

9:00 ¹ ___English___ : write a story

10:00 ² _____________ : learn about plants

11:00: ³ _____________ with students in Canada!

Today's ⁴ _____________ : read pages 11–13, do two math problems

B **Circle the correct option.**

1 A: Do you have **science** / (**English**) class today?

   B: No, I don't.

2 A: Do you have **science** / **math** class now?

   B: Yes, we do!

3 A: Do you **homework** / **talk** to the students in Mexico every Wednesday?

   B: Yes, we do! It's my favorite day.

4 A: Do you have English **homework** / **video chat** for tomorrow?

   B: No, I don't. I have **English** / **math** homework.

A Circle the correct option.

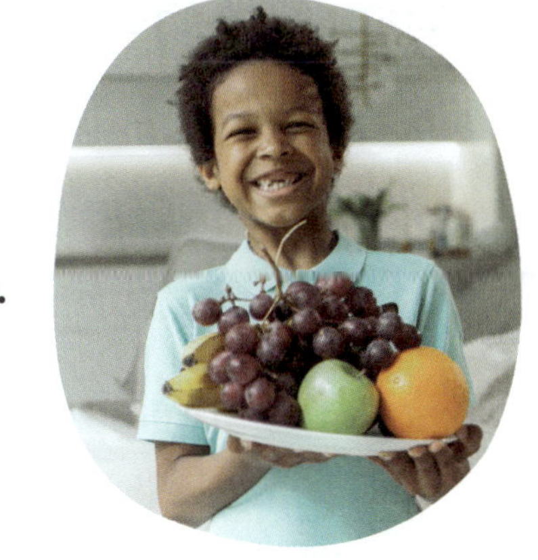

1 I like apples **and** / **but** grapes.

2 He likes seafood, **and** / **but** he doesn't like meat.

3 She wants cookies, **and** / **but** she doesn't want a cake.

4 You drink juice **and** / **but** water.

5 They eat chicken **and** / **but** vegetables.

B Complete the sentences with *and* or *but*.

1 I like making models, _______**but**_______ I don't like board games.

2 We have fun in science class _______________ math class.

3 They like riding horses _______________ playing with cats.

4 He climbs buildings, _______________ he doesn't climb mountains.

5 She visits her grandparents _______________ her cousins.

C Join the sentences with *and* or *but*.

1 I like vegetables. I don't like chicken.

   I like vegetables, but I don't like chicken.

2 She wants a sandwich. She wants a salad.

   ____

3 Olga travels by horse. Lea travels by boat.

   ____

4 They learn science. They learn English.

   ____

A Complete the chart.

English   meat   science   talk   seafood   climb

School Subjects	Food	Things People Do
English		

B Write the words in the correct order to make questions. Then write answers.

Yes, I do.   No, they don't.   Yes, they do.

1 movies / you / Do / like / ?

A: ___________________________________

B: ___________________________________

2 climb / Do / they / the mountain / ?

A: ___________________________________

B: ___________________________________

3 they / by boat / Do / travel / ?

A: ___________________________________

B: ___________________________________

Unit 9 and Me

My learning in this unit

I know about ___________________________________.

I want to know about ___________________________________.

10 How do people communicate?

Vocabulary 1

A Look and write the word.

feet   jump   hug   arms   shout   grumpy

1 _______________
2 _______________
3 _______________
4 _______________
5 _______________
6 _______________

B Circle the correct option.

1 I **sing** / **wake up** at 7:00 every day.

2 I open this present and **frown** / **smile**.

3 I open this present and **frown** / **smile**.

4 I like to **shout** / **sing** for my parents.

A Complete the chart.

He ~~I~~ It She They We You

... have eggs.	... has eggs.
I	_______
_______	_______
_______	_______
_______	

B Complete the sentences with *has* or *have*.

1 She _____ has _____ a ball.

2 I _______________ cookies.

3 They _______________ uniforms.

4 You _______________ a horse.

5 He _______________ a plate.

6 We _______________ instruments.

 Circle the correct option.

1 We **do not** / **does not** have homework.

2 She **do not** / **does not** have a brother.

3 You **don't** / **doesn't** have a rabbit.

4 I **don't** / **doesn't** have a pencil.

5 He **don't** / **doesn't** have cookies.

6 They **don't** / **doesn't** have books.

D **Look and complete the sentences.**

1 She ____doesn't have____ apples.

2 They __________________ salads.

3 He __________________ water.

4 It __________________ meat.

5 You __________________ a pencil, but I __________________ a pencil for you.

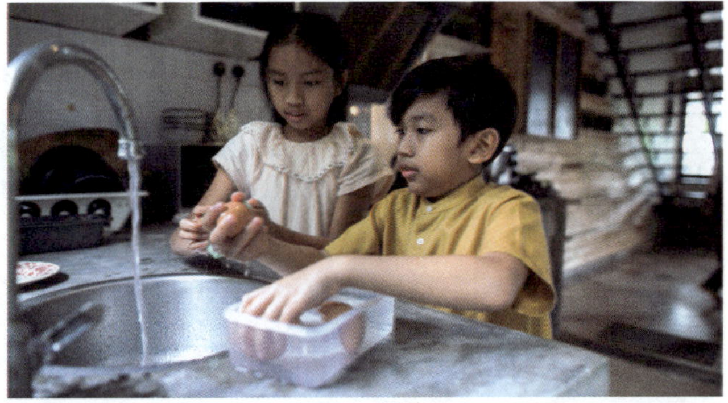

6 We __________________ chickens, but we __________________ eggs!

A Read the story. Who makes Victoria smile?

Victoria Is GRUMPY!

It's 7:00 on Monday morning. Victoria wakes up. She has school today. She's grumpy!

Victoria's dad makes eggs for breakfast. Victoria doesn't like eggs. She frowns.

Victoria goes to school. Saffi is in Victoria's chair talking to Lionel. Victoria wants to sit down. She's angry.

Victoria sits at a different table. She looks in her bag, but she doesn't have a pencil. She crosses her arms. This is a bad morning!

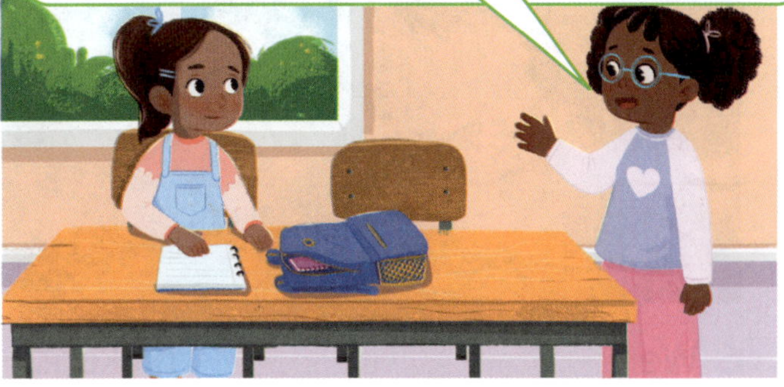

Saffi sees Victoria and goes to the table.

Victoria smiles. The morning is good now!

wakes up   grumpy   frowns   arms   smiles

C Number the pictures in the correct order.

a Victoria eats eggs for breakfast.

b Victoria doesn't have a pencil.

c Victoria wakes up.

d Saffi is in Victoria's chair.

D Match the causes to the effects.

Cause

1 Victoria has school today.

2 Victoria's dad makes eggs.

3 Saffi is in Victoria's chair.

4 Victoria doesn't have a pencil.

5 Saffi comes to Victoria's table.

Effect

a Victoria is angry.

b Victoria wakes up at 7:00.

c Victoria frowns.

d Victoria smiles.

e Victoria crosses her arms.

What makes you smile?

A Look and write the word.

hands   body   face

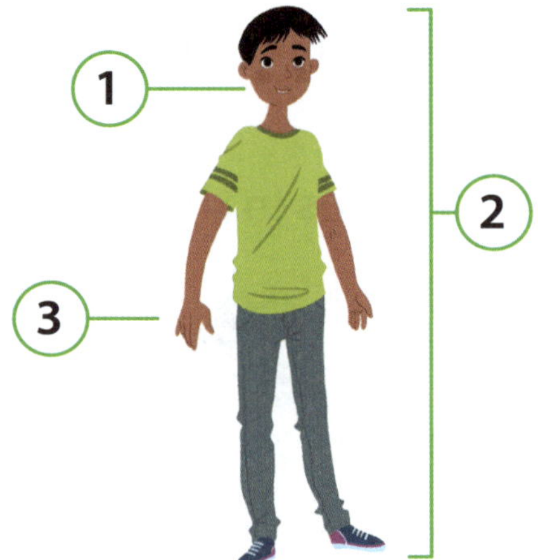

1 ___________________

2 ___________________

3 ___________________

B Read and complete.

hear   sign language   hands   camping

Hi! I'm Ivy, and this is my family. This weekend, we are ¹ ___________________ !
My sister, Kimi, can't ² ___________________ . So, we communicate with
³ ___________________ . This means we use our ⁴ ___________________ to talk.
Tonight, we're telling stories around our campfire. It's fun!

Do you like camping? Why? / Why not?

A Match.

1 lifeguard

a

2 paramedic

b

3 server

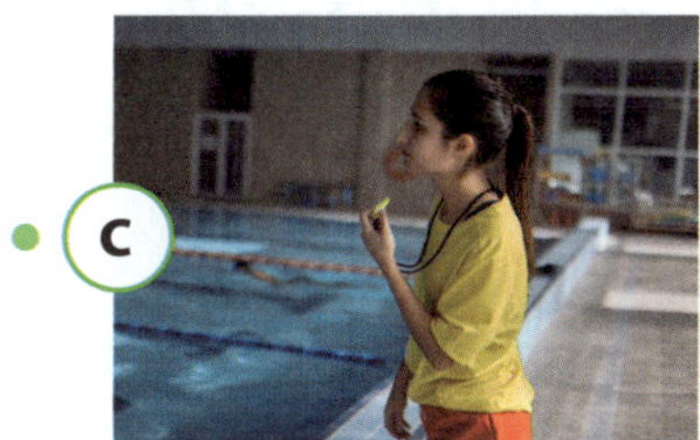
c

B Who works at these places? Write the numbers from A.

a

b

c

C Complete the sentences.

siren   lifeguard   whistle   paramedic   server   writes

1 A _________________ travels to help people.

2 A _________________ gets people the food they want.

3 A police car has a _________________ to tell other cars to move.

4 A soccer coach has a _________________ to get the team to listen.

5 A _________________ keeps people safe at the swimming pool.

6 A teacher _________________ sentences for students to read.

A Match.

1 a noun   **a** a person, place, or thing

2 a verb   **b** tells us more about a person, place, or thing

3 an adjective   **c** an action word

B Look at the underlined words. Write *N* for noun, *V* for verb, or *A* for adjective.

1 The server works in a <u>café</u>.   <u>N</u>

2 He <u>writes</u> what the mom and daughter want to eat.   ___

3 The mom has a <u>big</u> bottle of water.   ___

4 The <u>daughter</u> has orange juice. ___

5 The daughter has a <u>red</u> T-shirt. ___

6 The three people <u>smile</u>. ___

C Complete the chart.

arms   jump   sing   grumpy   warm   shout   body   siren   loud

Nouns	Verbs	Adjectives

A Cross out (X) the one that doesn't belong.

1 lifeguard — server — sign language

2 feet — frown — smile

3 arms — camping — face

4 shout — sing — siren

5 body — grumpy — hands

B Complete the sentences with *have, don't have, has,* or *doesn't have.*

1 She ___________________ a whistle.

2 He ___________________ a hat.

3 They ___________________ bags.

4 She ___________________ a water bottle.

5 They ___________________ books.

Unit 10 and Me

My learning in this unit

I know about ____ .

I want to know about ___________________________________ .

11 Why do living things communicate?

Vocabulary 1

A Look and circle the correct option.

1 **hungry** / **dirty**
2 **coat** / **ladder**
3 **sleep** / **bread**
4 **sleep** / **hungry**
5 **bread** / **dirty**
6 **coat** / **ladder**

B Check (✓) the correct option.

1 ☐ I'm hungry.
  ☐ I need a hat.

2 ☐ He has a bath before bed.
  ☐ He has dinner before bed.

3 ☐ They cry.
  ☐ They sleep.

4 ☐ They have dinner at home.
  ☐ They eat a lot of bread.

A Check (✓) the correct answer.

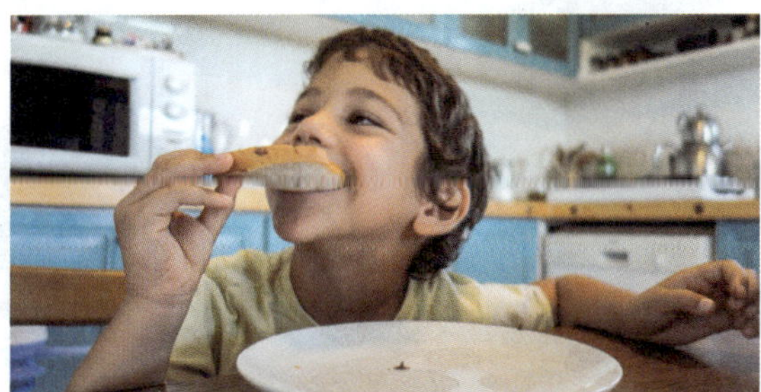

1 Does he eat bread?

- ☐ Yes, he does.
- ☐ No, he doesn't.

2 Does she need a coat?

- ☐ Yes, she does.
- ☐ No, she doesn't.

3 Does the town have a café?

- ☐ Yes, it does.
- ☐ No, it doesn't.

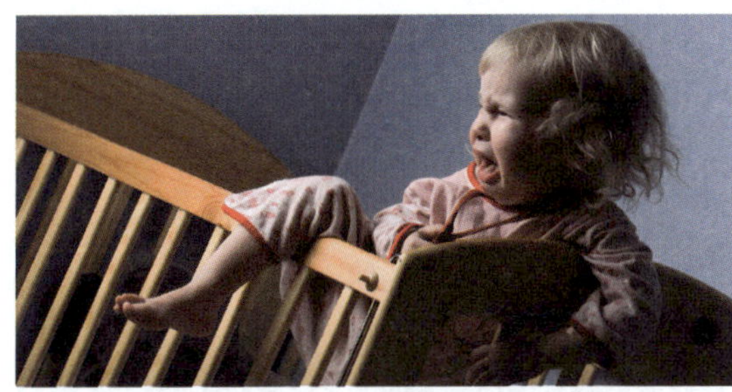

4 Does she want to sleep?

- ☐ Yes, she does.
- ☐ No, she doesn't.

B Write the words in the correct order to make questions.

1 want / dinner / Does / he / ?

____

2 Does / hungry / she / feel / ?

____

3 need / a bath / it / Does / ?

____

4 Does / he / baseball / play / ?

____

 Look and answer the questions.

1 Does she drink juice?

Yes, she does.

2 Does she need water?

3 Does he feel hungry?

4 Does she want the sandwich?

5 Does he like bread?

D **Complete the questions and answers.**

1 A: _____Does_____ he _____want_____ a cookie? (want)

B: Yes, _____he does_____ .

2 A: ______________ she ______________ to sleep? (need)

B: Yes, ______________ .

3 A: ______________ Mr. Lee ______________ this class? (teach)

B: No, ______________ .

4 A: ______________ the cat ______________ milk? (like)

B: Yes, ______________ .

5 A: ______________ your sister ______________ you study? (help)

B: No, ______________ .

6 A: ______________ the turtle ______________ in the ocean? (live)

B: No, ______________ .

A Read the story. Who helps Jack?

Jack Needs Jill

Jack and Jill go to the forest
to see what they can find.
Jack hears a sound and starts to cry.
Jill is calm and kind.

Does Jack need help?
Yes, he does!

Jack and Jill go to the beach
to have fun in a boat!
Jack sees his hat, but he can't swim.
Jill helps him with her coat.

Does Jack need help?
Yes, he does!

Jack and Jill are very hungry.
They sit to eat some bread.
Jack is tired and goes to sleep.
Jill puts him in his bed.

Does Jack need help?
Yes, he does!

cry   need   coat   bread   sleep

C Complete the sentences with *Jack* or *Jill*.

1 _____Jack_____ starts to cry.

2 _____________ is calm and kind.

3 _____________ can't swim.

4 _____________ uses a coat to help.

5 _____________ goes to sleep.

D Match the problems to the solutions.

Problems

1 Jack hears a sound and starts to cry.

2 Jack sees his hat in the water.

3 Jack and Jill are hungry.

4 Jack is tired and goes to sleep.

Solutions

a They sit to eat some bread.

b Jill puts him in his bed.

c Jill is calm and kind.

d Jill helps him with her coat.

Who do you ask for help? Why?

 ## Vocabulary 2

A **Match.**

1 bee

2 grow

3 root

4 young

5 old

6 food

a

b

c

d

e

f

B **Write the letters to complete the words in the sentences.**

1 The black rabbit is **o** _l_ _d_ and likes to sleep.

2 The baby rabbit is **yo** __ __ __ and likes to play.

3 The baby rabbit __ __ **o** __ **s** every week.

4 The rabbits eat **f** __ __ __ in the morning.

5 The baby rabbit wants to see the __ **e** __ that's next to the flower.

6 The baby rabbit plays in the __ __ __ **ts** of the tree.

A Look and write the word.

leopard   dolphin   nest   snake   monkey

1 _______________

2 _______________

3 _______________

4 _______________

5 _______________

B Circle the correct option.

1 **Dolphins** / **Monkeys** need trees to be safe.

2 **Leopards** / **Nests** need meat to eat.

3 **Sounds** / **Snakes** need the sun to warm their bodies.

4 **Dolphins** / **Leopards** need to live in water.

5 Birds need **nests** / **snakes** for their babies.

6 Dolphins make loud **monkeys** / **sounds** to communicate.

Which animal from A is your favorite? Why?

11 Word Study

A Match to make sentences.

1 The baby cries …

2 The boy needs a bath …

3 The girl's hands are dirty …

4 My sister wants bread …

5 Mrs. Snow is tired …

a because he's dirty.

b because he needs to sleep.

c because she has many children.

d because she's hungry.

e because she likes painting.

B Join the sentences with *because*.

1 The dolphin makes a sound. It wants to communicate.

The dolphin makes a sound because it wants to communicate.

2 The leopard drinks water. It's thirsty.

____

3 The bee flies to the flower. It's hungry.

____

4 The bird makes a nest. It wants to have babies.

____

C Complete the sentences about you.

1 I want _________________ because _________________ .

2 I need _________________ because _________________ .

A Write the words in the correct groups.

monkey   bread   dirty   grow

1 dinner, food, _______________

2 dolphin, leopard, _______________

3 cry, sleep, _______________

4 hungry, old, _______________

B Correct the questions.

1 Does the boy likes the bath?

Does the boy **like** the bath?

____

2 Do the leopard make a sound?

____

____

3 Does the bird has a nest?

____

____

4 Do the girl need a coat?

____

____

Unit 11 and Me

My learning in this unit

I know about _______________.

I want to know about _______________.

Vocabulary 1

A **Complete the sentences.**

> ants   ground   danger   underground   collect

1 These animals are _______________.

2 They're going _______________.

3 They _______________ food every day.

4 These ants live in a nest on the _______________.

5 Look! There's an anteater. Now they're in _______________!

B **Circle the correct option.**

1 Leopards use their **protects** / **senses** to find other animals.

2 Leopards use their **noses** / **dangers** to **collect** / **smell** other animals.

3 Leopards know the **scents** / **noses** of different animals that they smell.

4 Leopards **ground** / **protect** their babies when there is **danger** / **an ant**.

A Check (✓) the correct option.

1 ☐ This is my English book.
 ☐ That is my math book.

2 ☐ This is my English book.
 ☐ That is my math book.

3 ☐ Those are my big sisters.
 ☐ These are my school friends.

4 ☐ Those are my big sisters.
 ☐ These are my school friends.

B Circle the correct option.

1 **This** / **These** are my cousins.

2 **This** / **These** is my pencil.

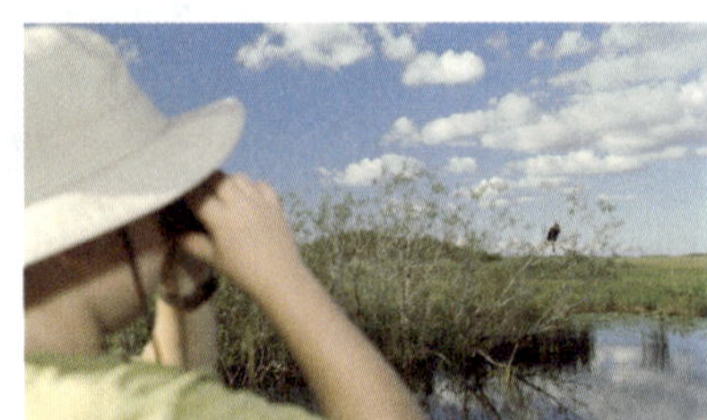

3 **That** / **Those** is a bird.

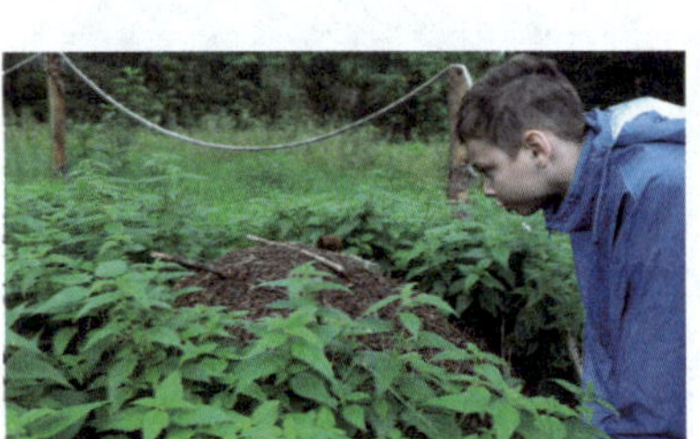

4 **That** / **Those** are ants.

5 **This** / **Those** is my rabbit.

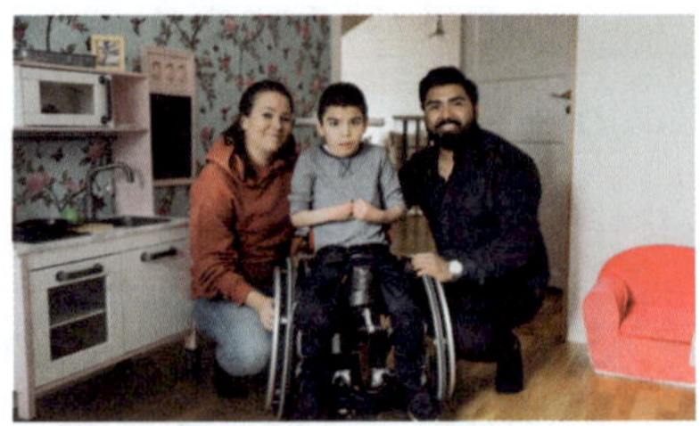

6 **That** / **These** are my parents.

 Complete the sentences with *This, That, These,* or *Those*.

1 _________________ ant is walking on my hand.

2 _________________ ants are going underground.

3 _________________ ant has an egg.

4 _________________ ants are protecting the nest.

 Look and complete the sentences. Use *This, That, These,* or *Those*.

1 _____*These squirrels*_____ are black, but _________________ are brown.

2 _________________ is jumping!

3 _________________ is beautiful!

4 _________________ are collecting food.

A **Read the story. What do dolphins like to do?**

Amazing Dolphins!

Dolphins live in the water. Most dolphins live in the ocean, but some dolphins live in rivers.

Dolphins like to communicate. They make sounds, like whistles, to "talk" to other dolphins. They also use their bodies. They jump and hit the water to communicate. This dolphin is jumping to show that it wants to play.

Dolphins have some good senses. Dolphins can see well above and under the water. These dolphins are looking for danger. Dolphins can also hear. They have small ears, but they can hear more than people.

What is one thing dolphins can't do? Smell! A dolphin's nose is on its head, but dolphins don't use their noses to smell.

B Underline these words in the text.

senses   danger   smell   nose

C Which word do you see in the text many times? Check (✓).

☐ danger   ☐ dolphins   ☐ nose   ☐ play

D Circle *True* or *False*.

1 All dolphins live in the ocean.		True	False
2 Dolphins use their bodies to communicate.		True	False
3 Dolphins jump to communicate.		True	False
4 Dolphins can see under the water.		True	False
5 Dolphins have big ears.		True	False
6 Dolphins use their noses to smell.		True	False

What do you think is amazing about dolphins? Why?

A Circle the correct option.

1 hit / touch   **2 clean / goat**   **3 head / hit**

4 touch / play   **5 goat / head**   **6 clean / touch**

B Look and write the number.

a [2] The girl touches the goat.   **c** [ ] The girl plays with the goat.

b [ ] The girl cleans the goat.   **d** [ ] This is the goat's head.

12 Vocabulary 3

A Look and write the letters to complete the words.

1 __ i __ h __

2 d __ __ o __ au __

3 __ ig __

4 __ l __ __ r

5 w __ __

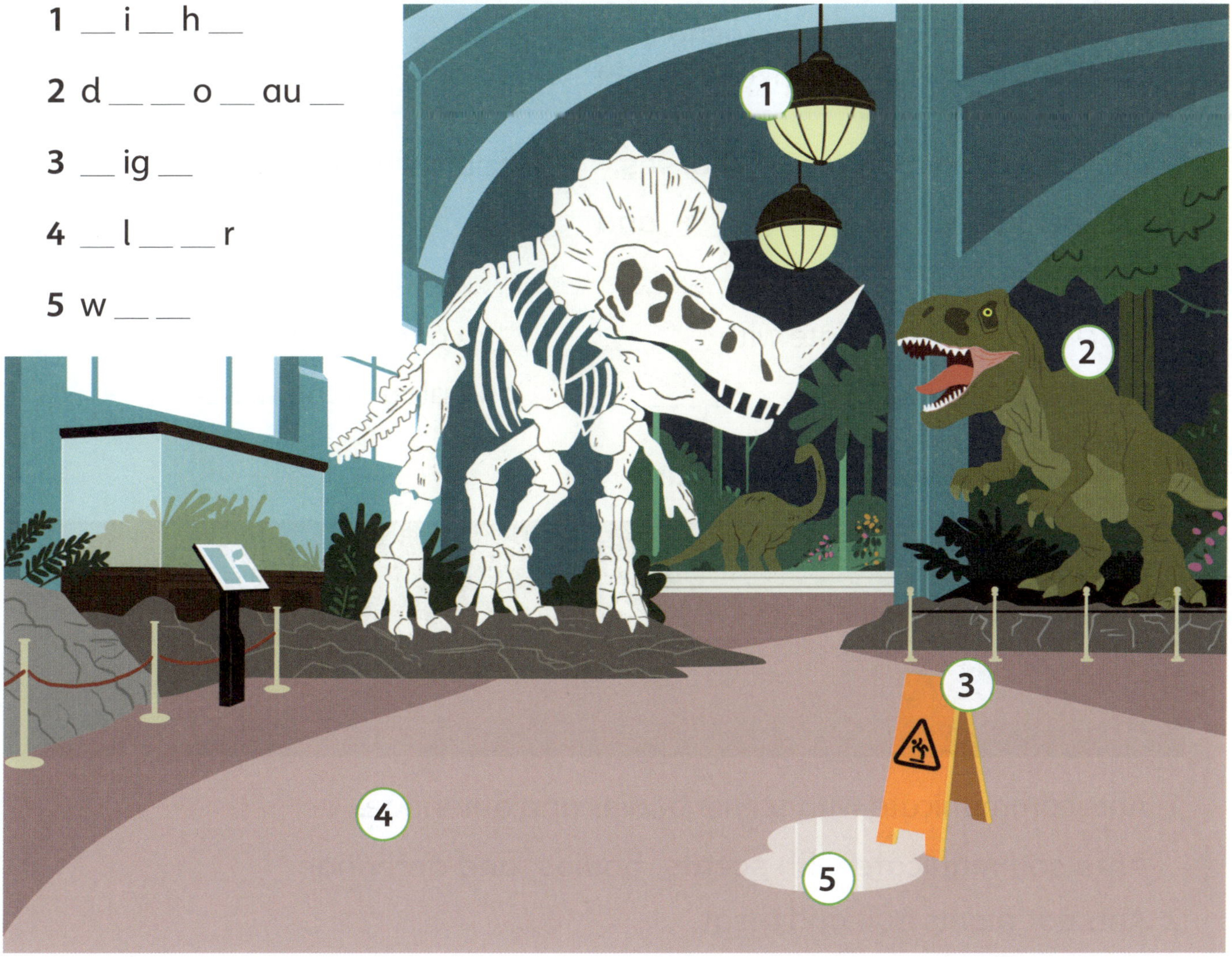

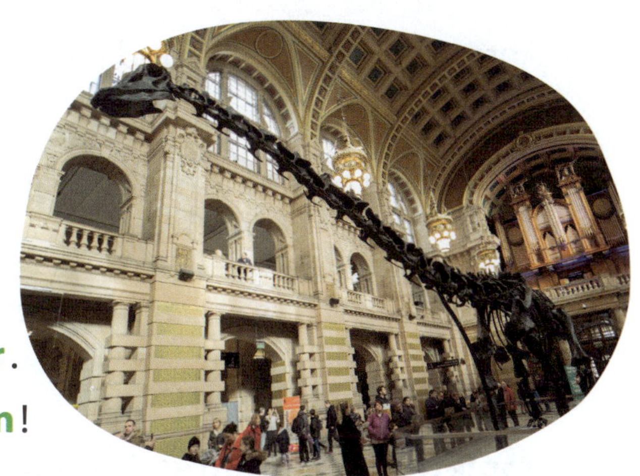

B Circle the correct option.

1 This is a big **dinosaur** / **sight**.

2 There is **light** / **wet** so people can see the dinosaur.

3 The dinosaur isn't **sign** / **wet**.

4 The people are on the **floor** / **dinosaur**.

5 The dinosaur is an amazing **sight** / **sign**!

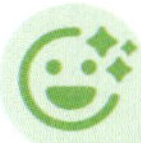

Do you like dinosaurs? Why? / Why not?

A **Complete the sentences and add commas.**

> bread   smell   hit   teachers   ~~horses~~
> students   jump   monkeys   sight   meat

1 My favorite animals are _____horses,_____ leopards, and _______________ .

2 I like to eat fruit, _______________ and _______________ .

3 I have senses of _______________ _______________ and touch.

4 At school I communicate with _______________ coaches, and _______________ .

5 Dolphins _______________ _______________ and play in the water.

B **Write the sentences with commas.**

1 Ants communicate with scents bodies and antennae.

Ants communicate with scents, bodies, and antennae.

2 Ants eat plants fruit and meat.

____

3 Ants drink water milk and juice.

____

4 Ants walk communicate and sleep underground.

____

5 I like ants because they're beautiful funny and amazing!

____

C **Complete the sentences. Use commas.**

1 My favorite animals are ____ .

2 I like to eat ____ .

A Cross out (X) the one that doesn't belong.

1 dinosaur   sense   sight
2 smell   touch   clean
3 collect   ground   protect
4 head   nose   sign
5 hit   play   underground
6 goat   wet   ant

B Complete the sentences with *This*, *That*, *These*, or *Those*.

1 _______________ dolphin is swimming in the ocean.

2 _______________ dolphins are in the river.

3 _______________ dolphins are playing.

4 _______________ dolphin is wet!

Unit 12 and Me

My learning in this unit   ☺   ☺   ☺

I know about _______________________________________.

I want to know about _______________________________.

Vocabulary 1

A Look and write the letters to complete the words.

Welcome to class!

These are ¹sh __ __ __ s!

²t __ __ an __ __ e

³ __ ir __ __ __ __

⁴ __ ec __ a __ __ le

⁵s __ __ a __ e

⁶ __ __ a __

B Complete the sentences.

numbers   count   even numbers   odd numbers

1 2 3 4 5
6 7 8 9 10

1 He can ________________ .

2 These are ________________ .

2 4 6 8 10

1 3 5 7 9

3 These are ________________ .

4 These are ________________ .

13 Grammar

A Match.

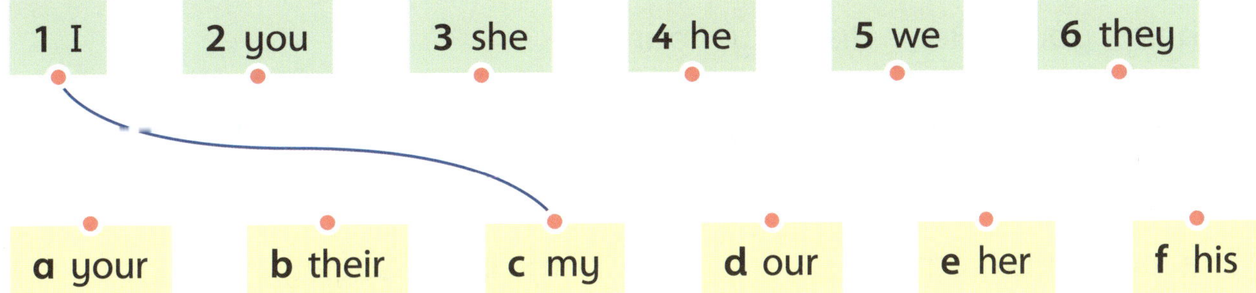

B Circle the correct option.

1 I'm Deniz. Come and meet **my** / **your** family.

2 This is my brother. **His** / **Our** name is Hasan.

3 This is my sister. **Her** / **His** name is Ella.

4 These are my parents. **Their** / **Your** names are Oluchi and Dilara.

5 That is **our** / **their** house. We live there.

6 Where does **my** / **your** family live, Parker?

C Complete the sentences.

Their   your   Her   His   My   our

1 I'm Esma, and I'm in first grade. _______________ favorite subject is math.

2 We have 20 students in _______________ class.

3 The teacher is great! _______________ name is Ms. Cayley.

4 My brother is in third grade. _______________ favorite subject is English.

5 My cousins are in fourth grade. _______________ school is nice, too.

6 Do you like math? What's _______________ favorite subject?

D Write the words in the correct order to make questions. Then match the questions to the pictures and write answers.

1 her / teacher / Is / kind / ?

____

____

2 Is / brother / your / happy / ?

____

____

a _______________________________

3 loud / music / their / Is / ?

____

____

b _______________________________

What's your favorite subject?

c _______________________________

A Read the story. What does Kalisha want to learn about?

Sharing ▶ Patterns

Antonio's class is learning about patterns in school.

Kalisha uses a star and a circle in her pattern.

Kalisha and Antonio make another pattern. They use even numbers.

B **Underline these words in the text.**

shapes   triangles   star   circle   even numbers

C **Categorize. Complete the chart.**

circle   ~~Kalisha~~   Ms. Lopez   star   triangle   Antonio

People	Shapes
Kalisha	

D **Circle the correct option.**

1 Antonio is learning about **colors** / **patterns** in school.

2 Kalisha **wants** / **doesn't want** to learn from Antonio.

3 A pattern is **a different** / **the same** thing again and again.

4 Kalisha makes a pattern with **numbers** / **shapes** .

5 Antonio and Kalisha make a pattern with **even numbers** / **odd numbers** .

A Look and write the letter.

1 line ___
2 sculpture ___
3 dot ___
4 wood ___
5 painting ___
6 mural ___

B Complete the sentences with words from A.

1 There's a ________________ of a tree.
2 The ________________ is blue.
3 The ________________ is black.
4 The ________________ has shapes in it.
5 The chairs are made from ________________.
6 The ________________ has people in it.

A **Look and write the word.**

beat   guitar   piano   difficult   fast   slow

1 ___________

2 ___________

3 ___________

4 ___________

5 ___________

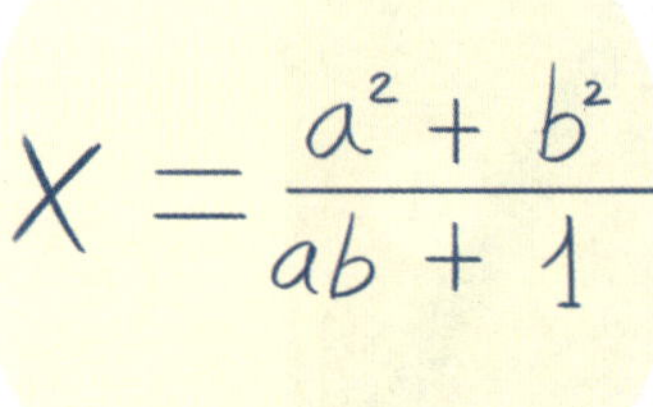

6 ___________

B **Circle the correct option.**

1 Music can have a pattern with a **beat** / **slow** .

2 Learning to play the guitar can be **difficult** / **piano** .

3 This **beat** / **piano** is big and black and white.

4 This music is **difficult** / **fast** ! I want to dance!

5 The music is **guitar** / **slow** and helps me sleep.

What instruments can you play?

A Match the numbers to the words.

1 20

2 22

3 30

4 70

5 100

a thirty

b one hundred

c twenty

d seventy

e twenty-two

B Complete the chart with the numbers or words.

1 _____21_____	**50**	3 __________	**88**
twenty-one	2 __________	sixty-three	4 __________
5 __________	**49**	7 __________	**37**
seventy-four	6 __________	ninety	8 __________

C Write the next word in the pattern.

1 twenty-four, twenty-five, ___twenty-six___

2 sixty-six, sixty-seven, __________

3 forty-one, forty-three, __________

4 thirty, forty, __________

5 eighty, ninety, __________

A Complete the chart.

beat   painting   square   star   guitar
mural   circle   piano   sculpture

Art Words	Music Words	Shapes
__________	__________	__________
__________	__________	__________
__________	__________	__________

B Complete the sentences.

her   Their   His   our   my

1 I'm Adem. These are ________________ friends.

2 ________________ names are Mei and Diego.

3 We play on a soccer team.
________________ team is The Ants.

4 Mei wears a different uniform.
________________ shirt is yellow.

5 Diego is very fast. ________________
favorite thing is running!

Unit 13 and Me

My learning in this unit   

I know about ____.

I want to know about ________________________________.

14 What patterns are there in nature?

A Look and write the word.

tail   wall   shell   notebook   pasta   spiral

1 _______________

2 _______________

3 _______________

4 _______________

5 _______________

6 _______________

B Read and complete.

yard   lizard   sheep   farm

I'm Christelle, and this is my ¹_______________,
Rocky. We live on a big ²_______________
with a lot of other animals. There's a small
³_______________ where Rocky can eat
and play. Sometimes this little green
⁴_______________ comes to visit!

14 Grammar

A Match.

1 Mo's lizard

2 Amadou's sheep

3 Ria's horse

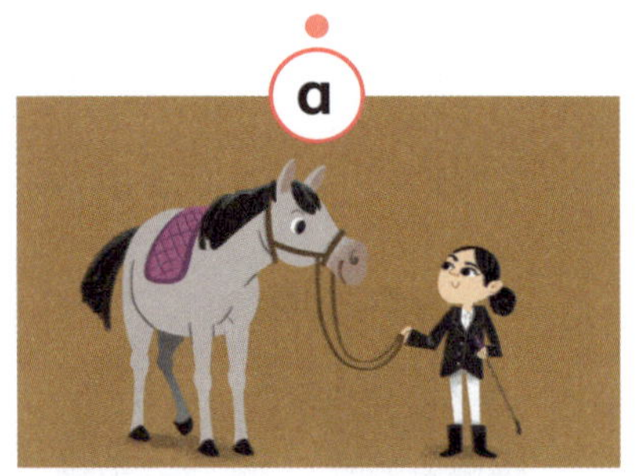

a

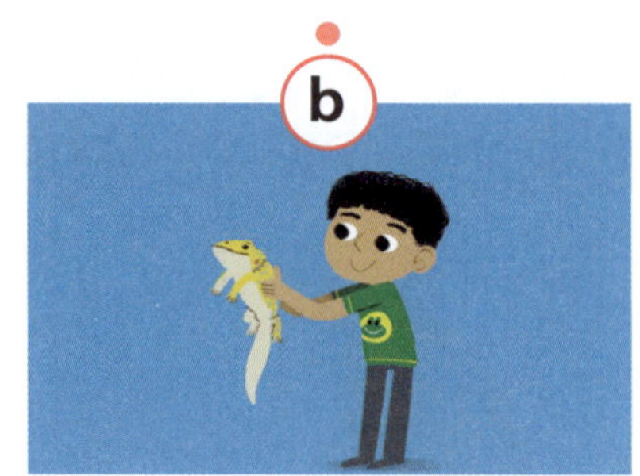

b

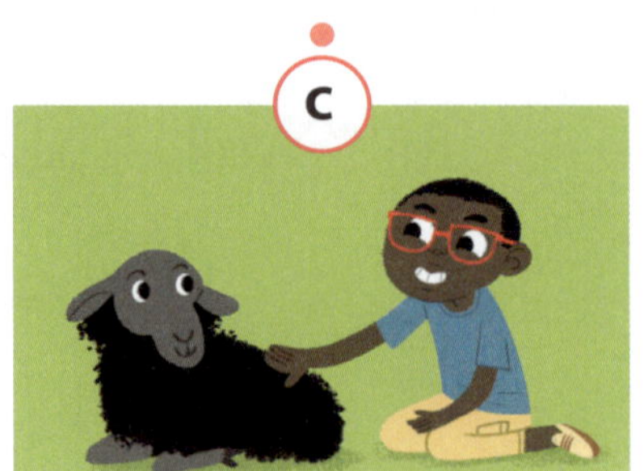

c

B Follow the lines and complete the sentences.

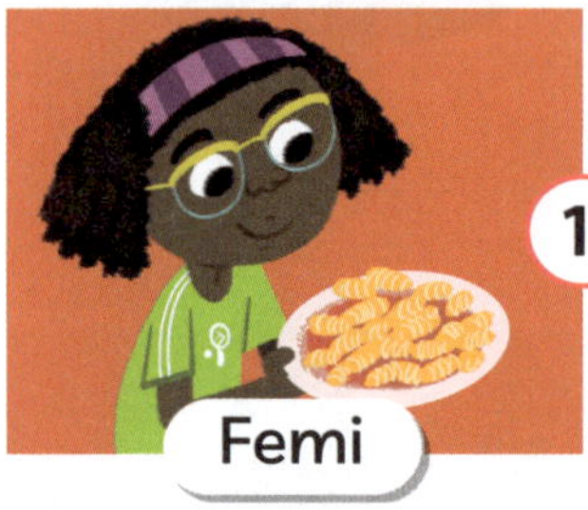
Femi

1

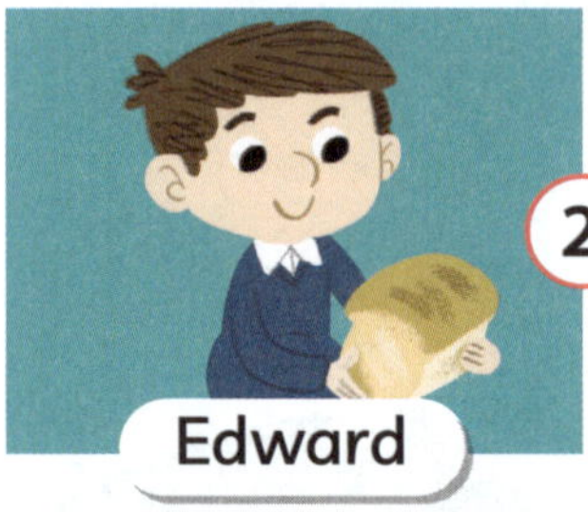
Edward

2

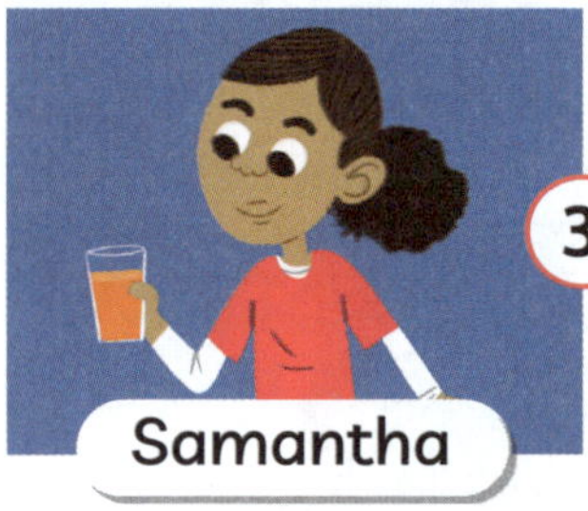
Samantha

3

a This is ____________ bread.

b This is ____________ sandwich.

c This is ____________ milk.

d This is ____Femi's____ pasta.

e This is ____________ juice.

4
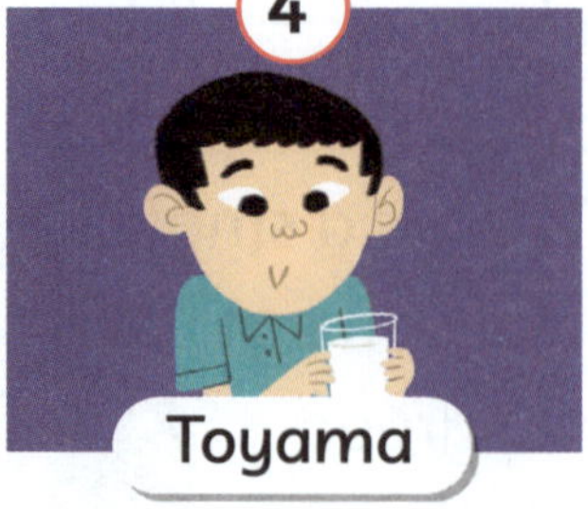
Toyama

5
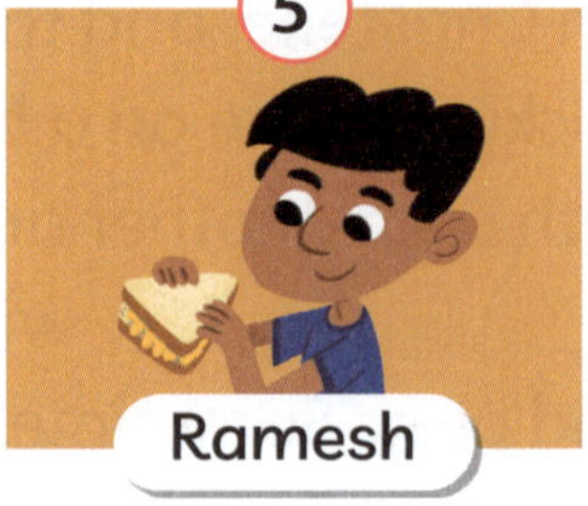
Ramesh

C Circle 's. Then complete the answers.

1 Is Amal**'s** book big? Yes, _____ it is _____ .

2 Is Mehmet's pencil yellow? No, _________________ .

3 Is Tadeo's bag new? _________________ , it is.

4 Is Margaret's notebook red? _________________ , it isn't.

D Write the words in the correct order to make questions. Then write answers.

1 blue / George's / Is / boat / ?

A: Is George's boat blue?

B: No, it isn't. His boat is black and white.

2 Is / Nandi's / small / car / ?

A: _________________________________

B: _________________________________

3 big / bear / Henri's / Is / ?

A: _________________________________

B: _________________________________

4 Jane's / Is / ball / green / ?

A: _________________________________

B: _________________________________

A **Read the story. What patterns do they see?**

Looking at Nature

Farez's family is driving to his aunt's house. The drive takes six hours, and Farez is tired. He wants to do something fun.

Farez's mom asks what he's learning in school. "Patterns!" says Farez.

"OK," says Farez's mom. "Let's look for patterns in nature."

"Great idea! I can write what we see in my notebook," says Farez.

"There!" says Farez. "The flowers have a pattern. Red, yellow, red, yellow."

"You're right," says Farez's dad.

"Oh, I see something!" says Farez's mom. "There's a lizard on the wall. Its tail has a pattern of black and green lines."

"Cool!" says Farez.

"We're here!" says Farez's dad.

"Wow!" says Farez. "Let's look for patterns again when we drive home!"

notebook   lizard   wall   tail

C ⚙ Number the events in the order they happen.

a 

b 

c 

d 

D Circle *True* or *False*.

1 Farez is going to visit his aunt.   True   False

2 The drive takes a long time.   True   False

3 Farez is learning about animals in school.   True   False

4 Farez's dad sees a lizard on a wall.   True   False

5 Farez wants to look for more patterns.   True   False

What animals do you know that have patterns?

A Look and write the letters to complete the words.

1 E _ _ _ h   2 li _ _ _   3 _ a _ _

  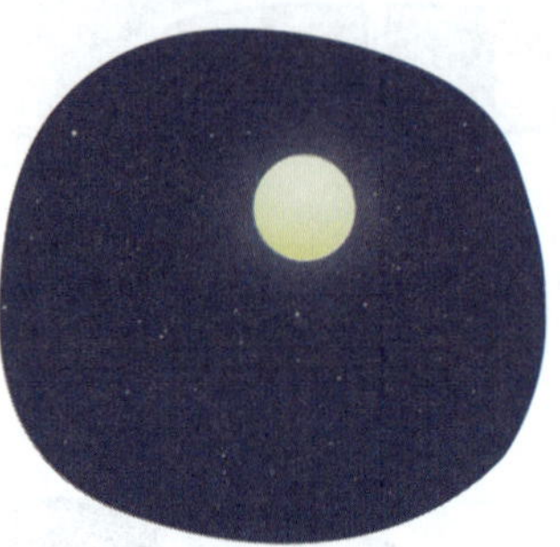

4 _ o _   5 m _ _ n _ _ g   6 n _ _ _ t

B Circle the correct option.

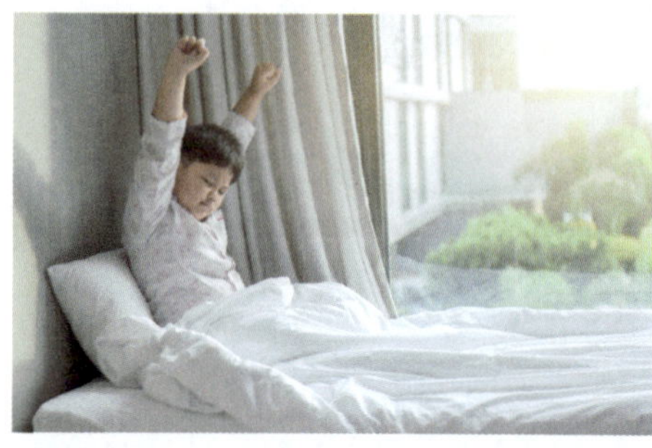

1 People usually wake up in the **morning** / **night** when it's **dark** / **light** outside.

2 People usually sleep at **morning** / **night** when it's **dark** / **light** outside.

What do you do in the morning? What do you do at night?

A **Look and write the word.**

heart   leaf   left side   butterfly   feather   right side

1 _____________

2 _____________

3 _____________

4 _____________

5 _____________

6 _____________

B **Circle the correct option.**

1 The **feather** / **heart** is on the water.

2 The **butterfly** / **leaf** is on the ground.

3 The **left side** / **butterfly** is on the flower.

4 The **heart** / **right side** is on the notebook.

A **Look at the underlined words. Circle *Noun* or *Verb*.**

1 The <u>butterfly</u> is colorful.

Noun   Verb

2 It <u>looks</u> beautiful.

Noun   Verb

3 It <u>likes</u> the flower.

Noun   Verb

4 It drinks <u>juice</u>.

Noun   Verb

5 It doesn't have <u>feathers</u>.

Noun   Verb

6 The butterfly <u>flies</u> away.

Noun   Verb

B **Match to make sentences.**

1 The park …   **a** come to the park.

2 There is …   **b** a playground here.

3 My friends …   **c** soccer on the grass.

4 We play …   **d** is a fun place.

C **Is it a complete sentence? Write *Yes* or *No*.**

1 That's a lizard.   Yes

2 The lizard small   __________

3 The lizard's tail is a spiral.   __________

4 It's green.   __________

5 lizard in nature   __________

A **Look and write the words.**

shell   heart   leaf   ~~butterfly~~   notebook   feather

1 _____butterfly_____ and   2 _______________ and   3 _______________ and

_______________   _______________   _______________

B **Write the words in the correct order to make sentences or questions.**

1 yard / Fatima's / is / This / .   _______________________________

2 house / blue / isn't / Marie's / .   _______________________________

3 Oli's / is / dark / bedroom / .   _______________________________

4 cold / Hiba's / Is / pasta / ?   _______________________________

5 tail / this fox's / Is / long / ?   _______________________________

Unit 14 and Me

My learning in this unit     

I know about ____.

I want to know about _______________________________________.

15 Why are patterns important?

A Circle the correct option.

1 The **fall** / **insects** are in the **grass** / **winter**.

2 The ants **grass** / **walk** on the leaf.

3 The dad and son go **north** / **winter** to see the mountain.

4 The mom and daughter go **fall** / **south** to see the river.

B Complete the sentences.

winter   fall   spring   die   summer

1 Many leaves _______________ in the _______________ .

2 In the _______________ , flowers grow and animals have babies.

3 Trees are green, and it's hot in the _______________ .

4 Some leaves change color in the _______________ .

A **Circle the correct option.**

1 The deer **can** / **can't** eat the leaves.

2 The birds **can** / **can't** drink the water.

3 The insects **can** / **can't** go up the tree.

4 The monkey **can** / **can't** get the fruit.

5 The goat **can** / **can't** climb up the mountain.

6 The baby birds **can** / **can't** fly.

B **Use *can* (✓) or *can't* (✗) to make sentences.**

1 Dolphins / swim / fast / . ✓

<u>Dolphins can swim fast.</u>

2 Sharks / fly / . ✗

____

3 Turtles / sleep / under the water / . ✓

____

4 Leopards / climb / trees / . ✓

____

5 Spiders / see / very well / . ✗

____

1 Can the bird fly?

☐ Yes, it can. ☐ No, it can't.

2 Can the duck swim?

☐ Yes, it can. ☐ No, it can't.

3 Can the fish walk?

☐ Yes, it can. ☐ No, it can't.

4 Can the deer climb the tree?

☐ Yes, it can. ☐ No, it can't.

D **Write the words in the correct order to make questions.
Then write answers.**

1 Can / catch the fish / the bird / ?

A: _______________________________________

B: _______________________________________

2 jump / the dolphin / Can / ?

A: _______________________________________

B: _______________________________________

3 swim / Can / the snake / ?

A: _______________________________________

B: _______________________________________

4 the crab / climb the rock / Can / ?

A: _______________________________________

B: _______________________________________

A Read the article. What ocean animals travel to different places?

Swimming to NEW PLACES

Birds and deer aren't the only animals that travel every year. Many sharks and sea turtles also travel to different places.

Great White Sharks

Great white sharks travel to have babies. They can't have babies in water that is too hot or too cold. They also want a safe place so their babies don't die. Great white sharks also travel to find food. They eat seals. Seals travel to look for fish to eat, and sharks travel to find the seals. Great white sharks can swim for thousands of miles to find food.

Green Sea Turtles

Green sea turtles also travel to have babies. They go to beaches to lay eggs out of the water. In Hawaii there are many green sea turtles. These turtles travel about 800 miles every summer to lay their eggs in Hawaii. Green sea turtles eat seagrass, and there's a lot of food in warm water. They travel north and south to find warm water.

C **Check (✓) *Great white shark* or *Green sea turtle*.**

1 This animal can't have babies in water that is too hot.

[ ] Great white shark   [ ] Green sea turtle

2 This animal lays eggs on beaches.

[ ] Great white shark   [ ] Green sea turtle

3 This animal can swim for thousands of miles.

[ ] Great white shark   [ ] Green sea turtle

4 This animal travels about 800 miles every summer.

[ ] Great white shark   [ ] Green sea turtle

D **Are they the same or different? Circle the correct option.**

1 Great white sharks have babies **in the water** / **on beaches**.

Green sea turtles lay eggs **in the water** / **on beaches**.

This is **different** / **the same**.

2 Great white sharks travel to **find food** / **sleep**.

Green sea turtles travel to **find food** / **sleep**.

This is **different** / **the same**.

3 Great white sharks eat **seagrass** / **seals**.

Sea turtles eat **seagrass** / **seals**.

This is **different** / **the same**.

A Look and write the letters to complete the words.

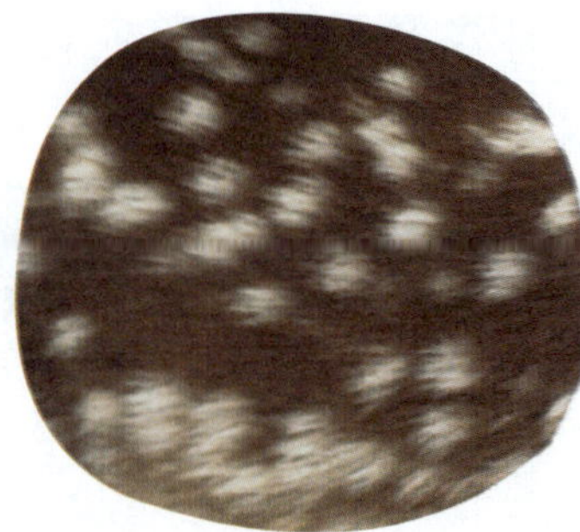

1 s __ __ ip __ s

2 __ e __ r __

3 s __ __ __ s

4 __ u __

5 __ __ d __

6 h __ __ __

B Complete the sentences with words from **A**.

1 A cheetah's dark ________________ help it ________________ from animals like lions.

2 Lions ________________ animals like deer.

3 Zebras have black and white ________________.

4 A rabbit's ________________ is usually brown or white.

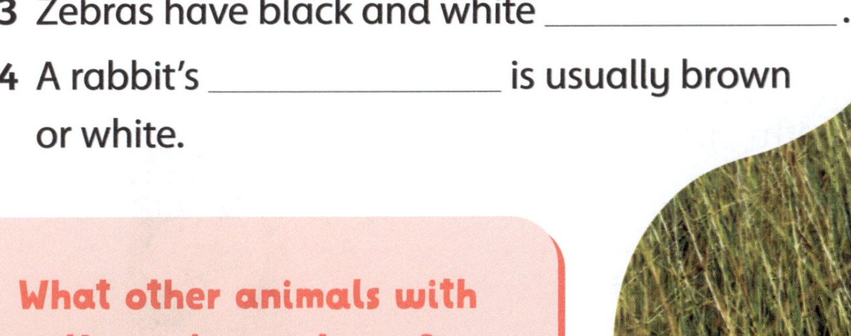

A **Check (✓) the correct option.**

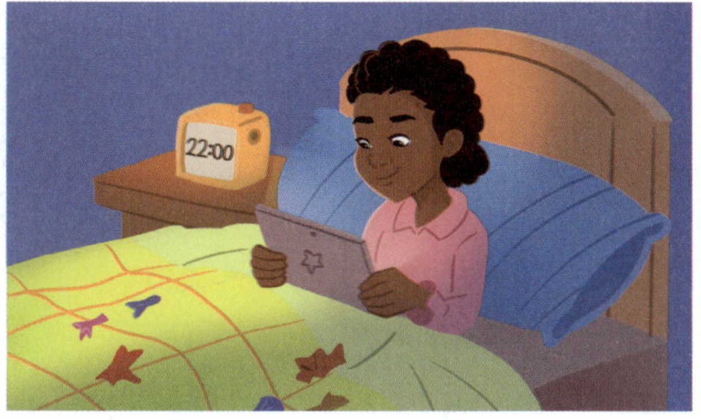

1 ☐ good
☐ bad

2 ☐ good
☐ bad

3 ☐ wash your hands
☐ brush your teeth

4 ☐ wash your hands
☐ brush your teeth

B **Read and complete.**

healthy   brushes her teeth   bad   habits

Maissa has some good ¹ _____________________
that she does every day. She eats a lot of
² _____________________ foods, like fruit and
vegetables. She doesn't eat too much candy
because it's ³ _____________________ for her
body. When Maissa eats candy, she always
⁴ _____________________ after she eats it!

15 Word Study

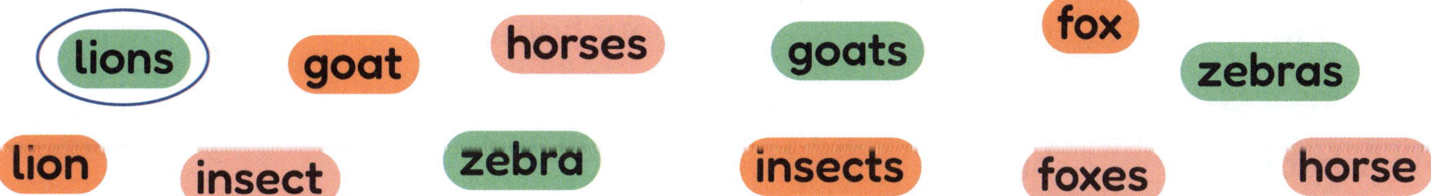

B Match the singular nouns to their plural ending.

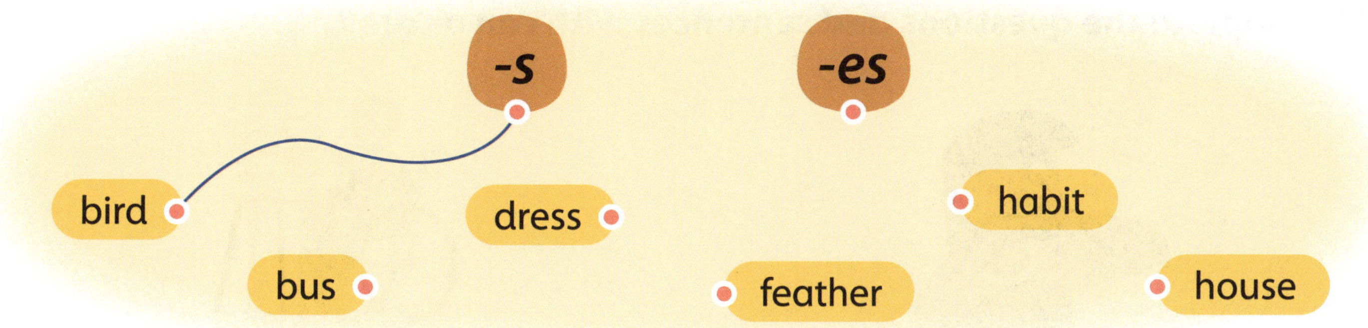

C Write the plurals.

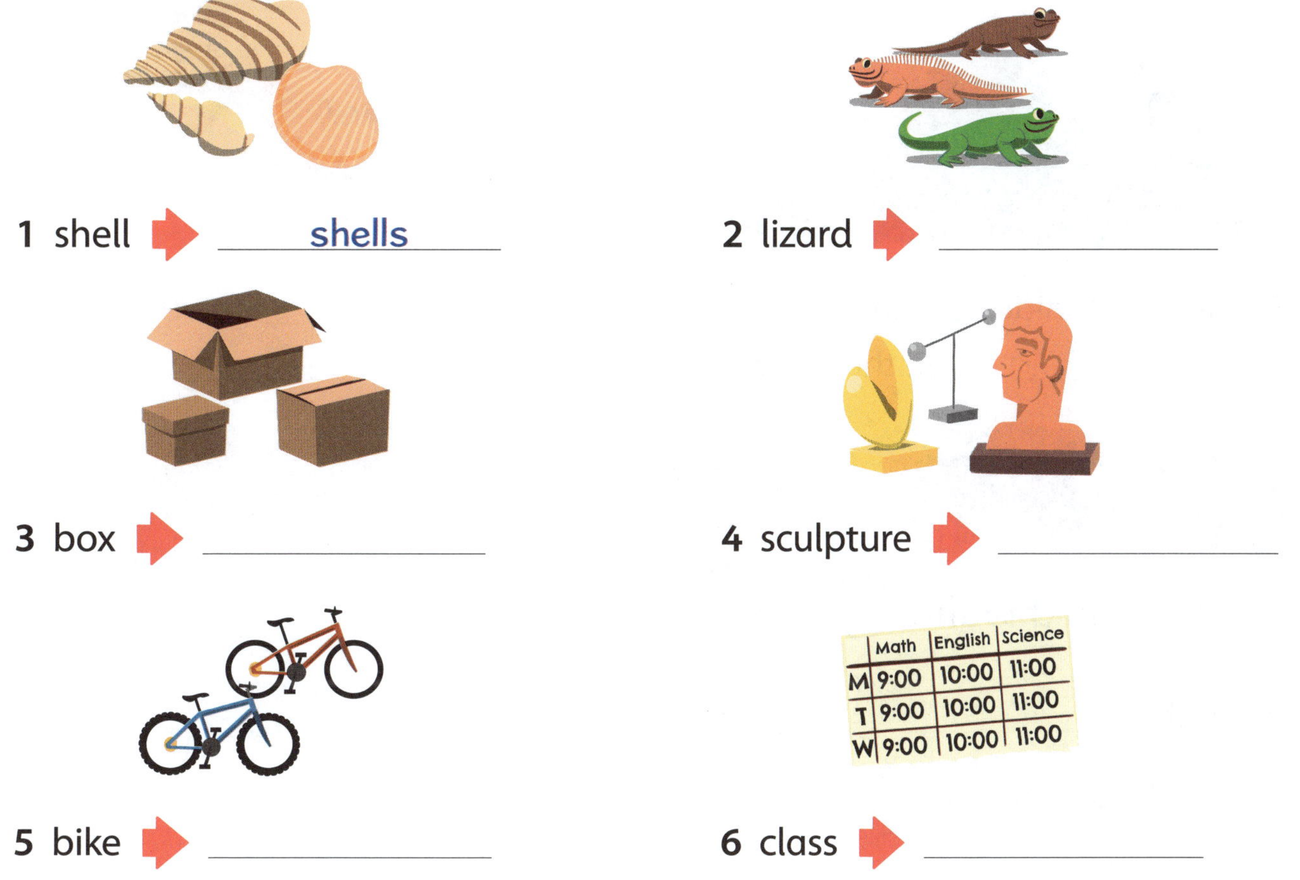

1 shell ➡ _____shells_____

2 lizard ➡ ________________

3 box ➡ ________________

4 sculpture ➡ ________________

5 bike ➡ ________________

6 class ➡ ________________

A **Cross out (*X*) the one that doesn't belong.**

1 bad   good   wash your hands

2 insects   grass   zebras

3 healthy   hide   walk

4 spots   stripes   winter

5 fall   north   south

B **Complete the questions and sentences with *can* or *can't*.**

1 Sarika ________________ brush her teeth.

2 ________________ Luc draw a lion?
Yes, he ________________ .

3 The rabbit hides. Lizzie ________________ see the rabbit.

4 ________________ Zawadi fly?
No, he ________________ .

Unit 15 and Me

My learning in this unit   

I know about ____ .

I want to know about ____ .

16 How can change happen?

A Look and write the word.

fall   windy   parent   garden   pumpkin

1 _______________

2 _______________

3 _______________

4 _______________

5 _______________

B Complete the sentences.

snow   poem   season   short   buds

1 This _______________ is spring.

2 He writes a _______________ about the summer.

3 The days are _______________ in the winter.
They play in the _______________ .

4 In the spring, many plants have _______________ .

A **Look and circle the correct option.**

1 **She's** / **She isn't** taking a photo of the bird.

2 **She's** / **She isn't** feeding the bird.

3 **He's** / **He isn't** painting.

4 **I'm** / **I'm not** working in the garden.

5 **He's** / **He isn't** helping his sister.

B **Check (✓) the correct option.**

1 ☐ They're playing soccer.

☐ They aren't playing soccer.

2 ☐ You're writing a poem.

☐ You aren't writing a poem.

3 ☐ We're eating snacks.

☐ We aren't eating snacks.

 Write the opposite sentences.

1 He's eating a pumpkin. <u>He isn't eating a pumpkin.</u>
2 She isn't having fun. _______________________
3 I'm not waiting for spring. _______________________
4 The leaves are falling. _______________________
5 The birds aren't flying. _______________________
6 I'm drawing a butterfly. _______________________

 Look and write the sentences.

1 (grow / a pumpkin) <u>She isn't growing a pumpkin.</u>

2 (sleep / in the garden) _______________________

3 (wear / big coats) _______________________

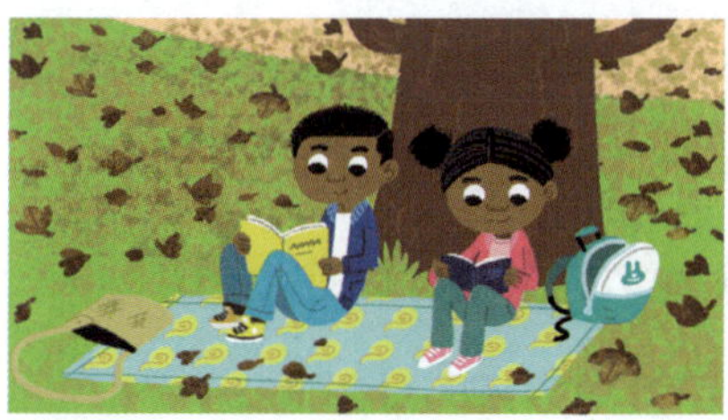

4 (write / poems) _______________________

5 (feed / the birds) _______________________

6 (fall / off the table) _______________________

What are you wearing today?

A Read the poem. What season is it?

The Beautiful Day

My name is Daniel. I live in Italy. We have different weather in every season. This is a poem about my favorite season.

The sun is shining.
It isn't windy today.
There are buds on the trees.
I'm ready to play.

Nature wakes up
here in the park.
The days aren't short.
It's sunny, not dark.

The plants are growing.
The park looks great.
Where are my parents?
They're standing by the gate.

The flowers are beautiful.
The birds all sing.
I'm smiling today
because it's spring!

B Underline these words in the text.

season   poem   buds   short

C Circle *True* or *False*.

1	The weather is nice.	True	False
2	It's cold and windy.	True	False
3	The trees have buds.	True	False
4	The days are short.	True	False
5	The plants are growing.	True	False
6	The birds are singing.	True	False

D What's the setting for the poem? Check (✓).

☐ a garden

☐ a park

☐ a forest

☐ a playground

What's your favorite season?

A **Look and write the letters to complete the words.**

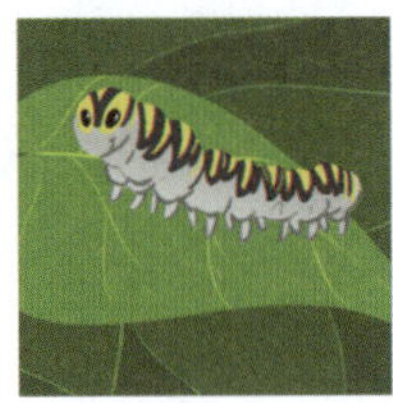

1 c __ t __ __ p __ __ __ ar

2 __ d __ __ t

3 i __ __ id __

4 __ g __

5 s __ __ o __ g

6 __ in __

B **Circle the correct option.**

1 A butterfly **adult** / **egg** becomes a **caterpillar** / **wing**.

2 A chrysalis is **inside** / **strong** to help the animal **inside** / **strong** be safe.

3 A big butterfly is an **adult** / **egg** and has two **caterpillars** / **wings**.

A **Look and write the letter.**

1 artist ___

2 freeze ___

3 ice ___

4 king ___

5 lake ___

6 melt ___

B **Cross out (X) the one that doesn't belong.**

1 artist   king   lake

2 freeze   artist   melt

3 snow   ice   king

4 river   lake   melt

C **Complete the sentences.**

king   artist   lake   ice

1 The _______________ draws a picture of a butterfly.

2 The _______________ on the mountain is melting.

3 The _______________ lives in a big castle.

4 The _______________ freezes in the winter.

A **Write the contractions.**

1 (She is) _______She's_______ his sister.

2 (He is) _______________ her brother.

3 (They are) _______________ in the garden.

4 (They are not) _______________ at the beach.

5 (What is) _______________ the season? Summer!

6 (You are not) _______________ in this garden.

B **Write the text using contractions for the bold words.**

[1] **I am** in a garden. [2] **It is not** a vegetable garden. [3] **It is** a beautiful flower garden. [4] **I am** helping a friend. [5] **That is** my friend's cat. [6] **It is** black and brown.

I'm ____

____

____

C **Write a sentence using each of the contractions.**

1 (I'm) ____

2 (they're) ____

3 (that's) ____

A Complete the chart.

artist   king   egg   ice   bud   parent

People	Things
____________	____________
____________	____________
____________	____________

B Look and write the sentences.

1 give water / to the pumpkin

He's giving water to the pumpkin.

2 sit / inside her house

____

3 have fun / in the snow

____

4 fall / to the ground

____

Unit 16 and Me

My learning in this unit   

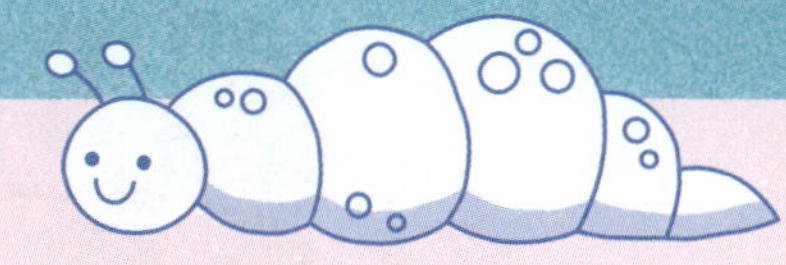

I know about ______________________________________.

I want to know about ______________________________________.

A Look and write the letter.

1 kitchen ___

2 money ___

3 plastic bottle ___

4 recycling bin ___

5 pencil holder ___

6 cut ___

B Complete the sentences.

use   reuse   throw away   seed

1 First, you ___________ the plastic bottle to drink.

2 Don't ___________ the bottle.

3 You can ___________ the bottle and make something new.

4 You can put bird ___________ in the bottle and make a bird feeder!

A Circle the correct option.

1 What **are** / **is** she making?

2 What **are** / **is** they using?

3 What **are** / **is** we making today?

4 What is he **reuse** / **reusing**?

5 What is she **cuts** / **cutting**?

6 What are you **do** / **doing**?

B Write the words in the correct order to make questions. Then write the letter of the answer.

1 What / doing / is / he / ?

What is he doing? __________ b

2 doing / is / she / What / ?

____

3 they / What / doing / are / ?

____

4 are / we / What / doing / ?

____

a She's giving seeds to the birds.

b He's making a bird feeder.

c We're playing soccer.

d They're playing in the park.

1 _________________ she eating cake?

☐ Yes, she is.   ☐ No, she isn't.

2 _________________ they having fun?

☐ Yes, they are.   ☐ No, they aren't.

3 _________________ he using a plastic bottle?

☐ Yes, he is.   ☐ No, he isn't.

4 _________________ it eating the seeds?

☐ Yes, it is.   ☐ No, it isn't.

D Read and complete.

getting   No   am   Are   ~~doing~~   What   making

Selim: Hi, Aya. What are you [1] _____doing_____?

Aya: Hi, Selim. I'm [2] _________________ a recycling bin.

Selim: Cool! [3] _________________ are you using?

Aya: We have a new TV at my house, and I [4] _________________ reusing its box.

Selim: Great idea! [5] _________________ you cutting the box?

Aya: [6] _________________ , I'm not. I want my recycling bin to be big. Hey! What are you doing?

Selim: I'm [7] _________________ my plastic bottle. I want to use your recycling bin!

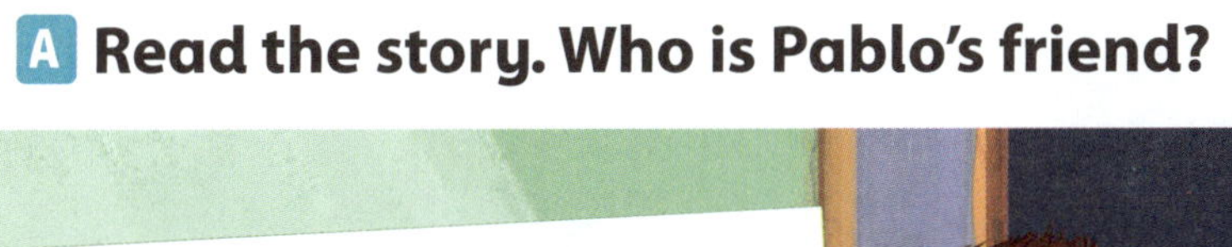

A **Read the story. Who is Pablo's friend?**

A Great Present

Pablo's friend Emma is moving to a new city. Pablo wants to give Emma a present to thank her for being his friend. Pablo goes to talk to his dad in the kitchen.

"Dad, I need something for Emma. Can you help me think of an idea?" asks Pablo.

"Sure," says Pablo's dad. "What does Emma like?"

"Well, she likes art. She also wants to help the Earth," says Pablo.

"OK. Maybe you can make something for her." says Pablo's dad.

"Cool idea! What are you doing with that plastic bottle?"

"I'm throwing it away."

"Don't throw it away! I can reuse it for Emma," says Pablo.

Pablo gets paint, scissors, and paper. His dad cuts the top off the bottle. Pablo cuts shapes from the paper and glues them on the bottle. Then he paints the bottle with different colors.

"Look!" says Pablo. "It's a pencil holder for Emma!"

"That's great, Pablo! She can use it in her new house!"

 Underline these words in the text.

kitchen   plastic bottle   reuse   cuts   pencil holder

 Match.

1 Pablo goes to the kitchen to talk to his dad.

2 Pablo makes a pencil holder.

3 Pablo's dad doesn't throw away his plastic bottle.

a beginning

b middle

c end

 Circle the correct option.

1 Emma is **making art** / **moving** to a new city.
2 Pablo asks his **dad** / **mom** for help.
3 Pablo says Emma likes **animals** / **art**.
4 Pablo says Emma wants to help **the Earth** / **Pablo**.
5 Pablo's dad wants to **reuse** / **throw away** the plastic bottle.
6 Pablo uses scissors, paper, and **paint** / **pencils** to make the pencil holder.

What can you reuse to make a present?

A **Complete the sentences.**

cuts down   bamboo   panda   park   road   builds

1 The ________________ is in the tree.

2 He ________________ the tree because it's too tall.

3 There's a lot of ________________ here.

4 The flowers are next to the ________________.

5 She ________________ a house.

6 They like playing in the ________________.

B **Match to make sentences.**

1 Pandas are special …   **a** build parks for pandas.

2 People build …   **b** bamboo that pandas eat.

3 People cut down …   **c** roads in places pandas live.

4 People can …   **d** animals.

A **Look and write the letters to complete the words.**

1 __ le __ __ up

2 __ __ as __

3 __ a __ __

4 k __ __ __

5 p __ __ __ __ up

B **Complete the sentences.**

kick   Pick up   ~~Clean up~~   Enjoy   trash

Park Rules

✔ **1** ___Clean up___ after your picnic.

✘ **2** Don't leave your ______________ in the park.

✔ **3** ______________ any old plastic bottles you see.

✘ **4** Don't ______________ the animals or plants.

✔ **5** ______________ your time here! ☺

A **Match the words to their plural forms.**

1 child   •   • **a** mice

2 mouse   •   • **b** tomatoes

3 tomato   •   • **c** children

4 sheep   •   • **d** potatoes

5 potato   •   • **e** sheep

B **Write the letter of the correct plural.**

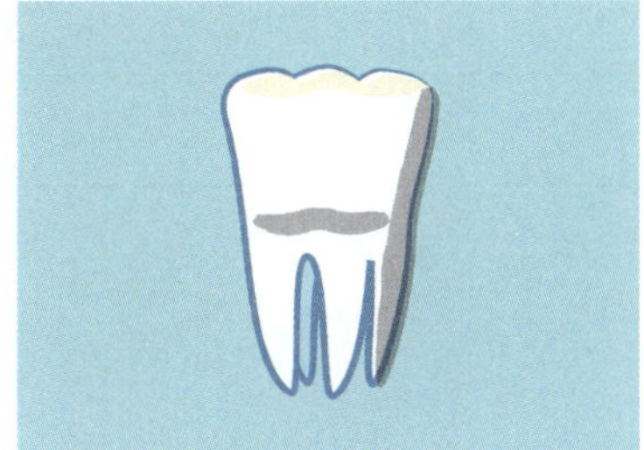  

1 tooth ___   2 foot ___   3 person ___

a    **b**    **c** 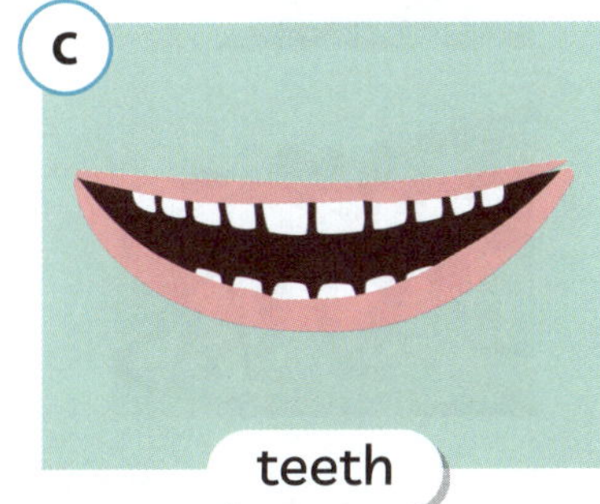

people   feet   teeth

C **Read and complete with words from A.**

The [1] ______child______ is watching
the [2] ________________ eating grass.
There are some [3] ________________
and a [4] ________________ in the bag.
The [5] ________________ are hiding behind
the wall.

A **Cross out (X) the one that doesn't belong.**

1 reuse	throw away	use
2 clean up	kitchen	pick up
3 kick	money	pencil holder
4 cut down	plastic bottle	recycling bin

B **Write the words in the correct order to make questions. Then write answers.**

1 she / give / seeds / to the birds / ?

A: Is she giving seeds to the birds?

B: Yes, she is.

2 they / make / a pencil holder / ?

A: _______________________________

B: _______________________________

3 What / he / cut / ?

A: _______________________________

B: _______________________________

4 What / they / do / ?

A: _______________________________

B: _______________________________

Unit 17 and Me

My learning in this unit   

I know about ____.

I want to know about _________________________________.

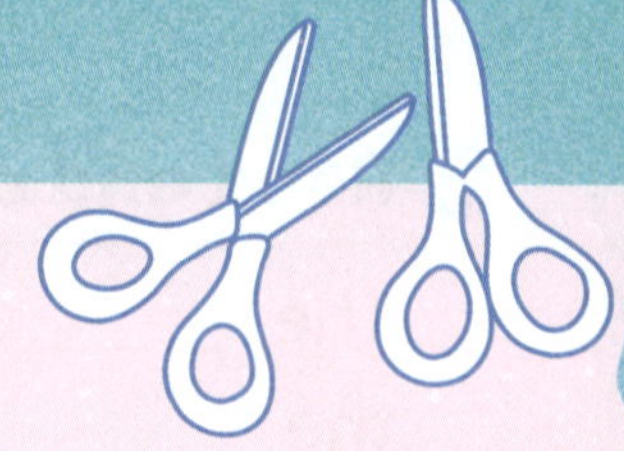

Vocabulary 1

A Complete the sentences.

> pushes   job   quiet   country   upstairs   neat

1 The house is in the ____________ .

2 He wants you to be ____________ .

3 She goes ____________ .

4 He ____________ the child.

5 Her bedroom is ____________ .

6 He likes his ____________ .

B Circle the correct option.

Linh: Hi Mai! I'm in my new [1] **apartment** / **upstairs**!

Mai: Cool! Can I see the [2] **country** / **view** from the windows?

Linh: Yes, look! We live on the top floor.

Mai: Does the building have an [3] **elevator** / **upstairs**?

Linh: Yes! It's a [4] **new** / **job** building. I like to [5] **quiet** / **push** the button.

Mai: Thanks for showing me your new home!

A Read and match.

1 

2 

3 

We always play soccer after school.

I sometimes see boats in the ocean.

He never uses the elevator.

a ✓✓

b ✗

c ✓✓✓✓

B Complete the sentences with *always*, *sometimes*, or *never*.

1 Her apartment is _______________ (✓✓✓✓) quiet.

2 Their house is _______________ (✗) quiet.

3 His rabbit _______________ (✓✓) wants to play.

4 Her lizard is _______________ (✓✓✓✓) sleeping.

Class 1A

	Monday	Tuesday	Wednesday	Thursday	Friday
9:00	Math	Math	Math	Math	Math
10:00	English	Gym	English	Gym	English
11:00	Science	Science	Science	Science	Science
12:00	Lunch	Lunch	Lunch	Lunch	Lunch
1:00	Gym	Art	Gym	Art	Gym

1 We **always** / **never** have math class at 9:00.

2 We **always** / **sometimes** have English class at 10:00.

3 We **sometimes** / **never** have lunch at 11:00.

4 We **always** / **sometimes** have science class at 11:00.

5 We **sometimes** / **never** have gym at 1:00.

6 We **always** / **never** have math class at 12:00.

D **Complete the sentences with *always*, *sometimes*, or *never*.**

1 I eat breakfast every day. I _____always_____ eat breakfast.

2 Breno eats eggs for breakfast on Mondays and Wednesdays.
Breno _______________ eats eggs for breakfast.

3 We don't like juice. We _______________ drink juice.

4 Mom says I can't ride my bike on the road. I _______________ ride
my bike on the road.

5 Azra does homework every day after school. Azra _______________
does her homework.

What do you always do in the morning?

A **Read the email. Where does Alyssa live now?**

To: Uncle Elmer x

August 11

Dear Uncle Elmer,

We are in our new apartment in Chicago! We have an elevator here! I like to push the buttons.

My bedroom is small, but it has a great view of the city. I like to sit and look out of the window. Sometimes it's loud in my bedroom, but it's fun to watch the cars at night. My room is always neat, too!

My brother, Jaden, also has a neat bedroom. His bedroom is big and quiet, but it doesn't have a good view. I like my bedroom the best.

My favorite thing about our new home is the swimming pool. Everyone in our apartment building can use it. It's upstairs on the top floor. It's the best!

I hope you can visit us soon.

Love,

Alyssa

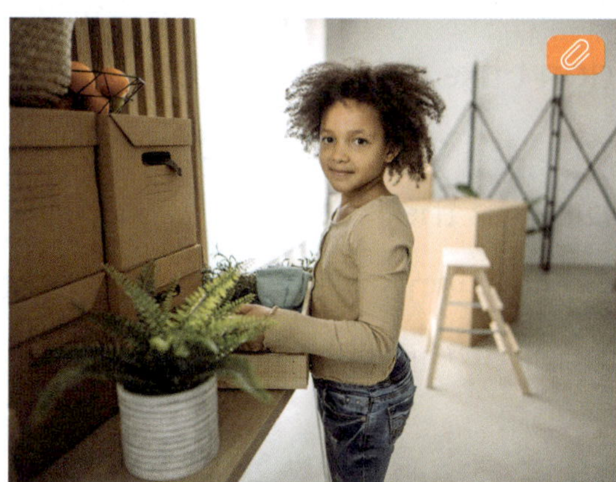

 Underline these words in the text.

new   apartment   elevator   push   view   neat   quiet   upstairs

 Circle the correct answer.

1 Which bedroom is small?

  a Alyssa's bedroom   **b** Jaden's bedroom   **c** both bedrooms

2 Which bedroom is big?

  a Alyssa's bedroom   **b** Jaden's bedroom   **c** both bedrooms

3 Which bedroom has a good view?

  a Alyssa's bedroom   **b** Jaden's bedroom   **c** both bedrooms

4 Which bedroom is neat?

  a Alyssa's bedroom   **b** Jaden's bedroom   **c** both bedrooms

5 Which bedroom is quiet?

  a Alyssa's bedroom   **b** Jaden's bedroom   **c** both bedrooms

6 Which bedroom is loud?

  a Alyssa's bedroom   **b** Jaden's bedroom   **c** both bedrooms

 Answer the questions.

1 Who is Alyssa writing to? ___________________________

2 Where is Alyssa's new apartment? ___________________________

3 What is Alyssa's favorite thing about the apartment? ___________________________

A **Look and write the letter.**

1 There's rain today. ___

2 This is a nice picnic. ___

3 They like to hike. ___

4 There's a storm in
   the country. ___

5 Nature is beautiful. ___

6 This is a little frog. ___

B **Read and complete.**

picnic   rain   hike   nature

Chadia likes to ¹________________ with
her dad. Chadia likes when it's sunny,
not when there's ²________________.
Sometimes Chadia and her dad take a
³________________ of sandwiches and
fruit to eat. Chadia likes everything
about ⁴________________ – the plants,
the animals, and the amazing views!

A **Look and write the word.**

apple   small   knees   ride   sneakers

1 _______________

2 _______________

3 _______________

4 _______________

5 _______________

B **Read and circle the correct option.**

Rafael and Joseph play on a baseball team together. They don't wear [1]**knees** / **sneakers**. They wear special baseball shoes called cleats. Rafael is holding his [2]**apple** / **knee** because it [3]**hurts** / **rides**. The ball is [4]**hurt** / **small**, but it's hard! Joseph asks if Rafael is OK.

Writing Study

A Match.

1 do not — c don't
2 does not — a doesn't
3 can not — b can't

B Complete the sentences with the contractions.

1 She (can not) ___can't___ find her sneaker.

2 He (does not) _________ use the elevator.

3 They (do not) _________ play on the same soccer team.

4 They (can not) _________ hike in the rain.

C Write a sentence using each of the contractions.

1 (can't) _______________________

2 (doesn't) _______________________

3 (don't) _______________________

A **Complete the sentences.**   quiet   hike   picnic   rain   storm   frog

1 The ________________ has a lot of ________________ .

2 They like to ________________ and stop for a ________________ .

3 The ________________ isn't ________________ . It's loud!

B **Complete the sentences with *always*, *sometimes*, or *never*.**

1 I eat apples for breakfast on Mondays. I ________________ eat apples.

2 Benito goes to the country every summer. Benito ________________ goes to the country in the summer.

3 We don't like spiders in the apartment. We ________________ want to see spiders in the apartment.

4 Tiwa's knee hurts when she walks upstairs, so she ________________ takes the elevator.

5 Zeki plays the piano on Tuesdays and Thursdays, but he doesn't play the piano on Mondays or Wednesdays. Zeki ________________ plays the piano.

Unit 18 and Me

My learning in this unit   

I know about ____ .

I want to know about ____ .

Writing Resource

Before you write

- Read the example text.

- Think about what it means.

- Think about your own ideas.

- Choose an idea to write about.

When you write

- Start your sentences with a capital letter.

- Use punctuation: commas, periods, and question marks.

- Write full sentences.

- Think about your spelling. Look in the dictionary if you don't know.

After you write

- Read your text.

- Correct your mistakes.

- Ask your friend or teacher to read your text.

M
~~my~~ name is Rosa.

I am seven.

family
My ~~famly~~ is big.

I have two sisters and three brothers.

Is your family big?

Checklist

I can check my work for:

- [✓] punctuation

- [✓] spelling

- [✓] full sentences

[✓] **I can correct my mistakes.**

Capital Letters

ABC Capital Letters for Names

The first letter of a name is a capital letter.

   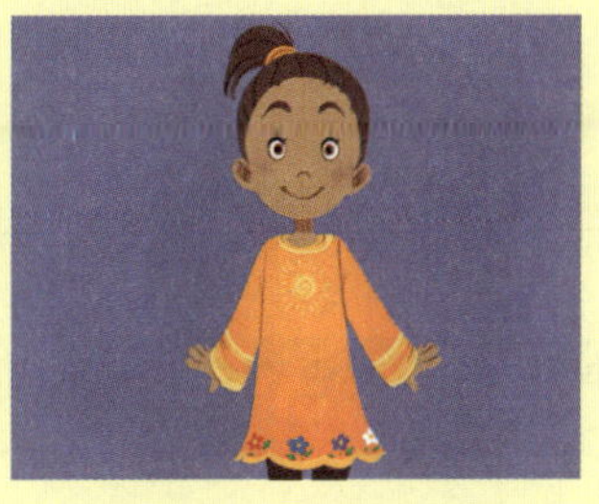

Alex **Carly** **Kashir** **Valentina**

ABC Capital Letters in Sentences

The first letter of a sentence is a capital letter.

There is a red seashell on the sand.

He has an orange hat.

Her name is Jenny. She's from Mexico.

Punctuation

. Periods

There is a period at the end of a sentence.

There is a red seashell on the sand.

He has an orange hat.

Her name is Jenny.

? Question Marks

There is a question mark at the end of a question.

Where is the frog?

Who's this?

What's that?

! Exclamation Points

Use an exclamation point to show strong feelings.

I love ice cream!

Let's go!

Be careful!

, Commas

Commas separate three or more words in a list.

There is a frog, a mouse, and a squirrel.

The flowers are yellow, purple, and pink.

My friends are Tom, Maria, Sofia, and Omar.

' Apostrophes and Possessive *s*

Use an apostrophe + *s* to show that something belongs to someone.

This is Luke's house.

That is Nada's cookie.

Where is Kate's backpack?

' Apostrophes and Contractions

Use an apostrophe when you make a contraction.

I am six.   I'm six.

You are my friend.   You're my friend.

She is a doctor.   She's a doctor.

It is summer.   It's summer.

It is not Saturday.   It isn't Saturday.

What is your name?   What's your name?

That is a lion.   That's a lion.

Parts of Speech

Nouns

Nouns are naming words. A noun is a person, place, or thing.

This is my sister.

I live in Egypt.

Where's your backpack?

Verbs

Verbs are action words.

Let's go!

I can jump.

We make apple pie.

Adjectives

Adjectives describe nouns. They tell you more about the nouns.

The statue is big.

It's a hot day.

Marco is lonely.

Subject-Verb Agreement

When you're writing, check that you have the correct form of the verb.

He was in the kitchen this morning.

They are very excited about the party.

We weren't hungry at lunchtime.

Complete Sentences

Nouns and Verbs

A complete sentence has a noun or nouns, and a verb in it.

The boy is hungry.

    noun verb

Ben goes to the park.

noun verb   noun

OXFORD
UNIVERSITY PRESS

Great Clarendon Street, Oxford, OX2 6DP, United Kingdom

Oxford University Press is a department of the University of Oxford.
It furthers the University's objective of excellence in research, scholarship,
and education by publishing worldwide. Oxford is a registered trade
mark of Oxford University Press in the UK and in certain other countries

ISBN: 978 0 19 486108 3   Blue Dot 1 Workbook

Printed in Spain by Indice, S.L.

This book is printed on paper from certified and well-managed sources

ACKNOWLEDGEMENTS

Illustrations by: Valeria Abatzoglu/Beehive Illustration, Flora Aranyi/Beehive
Illustration, Dalia Awad/Illustration X, Alejandra Barajas/Advocate, Elif
Balta Parks/Advocate, Martyn Cain/Beehive Illustration, Begona Fernandez
Corbalan/Advocate, Lidia Fernandez/Advocate, Barbara Gyuricza/Beehive
Illustration, Wendy Leach/Astound, Daniel Limon/Beehive Illustration,
Damien Jones/Illo Agency, Kaley McCabe/Advocate, Veronica Montoya/
Advocate, Nat Rivera/Advocate, Mark Ruffle, Valentina Toro/Advocate, Carlos
Velez Aguilera/Astound, Gareth Williams/Advocate.

Cover images by: Shutterstock (artjazz, Avesun, Jag_cz, Kitsana1980,
piyaphong, Vandathai).

Commissioned Photography by Will Amlot.

*The publisher would like to thank the following for their permission to
reproduce photographs*: Alamy Stock Photo (Alex Segre, AMELIE-BENOIST/
BSIP SA, Cliff Hide General News, Jeff Rotman, Kevin Schafer/Avalon.red,
Leonid Iastremskyi/Pixel-shot, Mariusika11, Paparazzi by Appointment,
Thomas Kitchin & Victoria Hurst/Design Pics Inc, USFWS Photo, Wavebreak
Media ltd, WILDLIFE GmbH); Getty Images (10'000 Hours/DigitalVision,
Aflo Images, Andersen Ross Photography Inc/DigitalVision, ARTindividual/
iStock, BJI/Blue Jean Images, borchee, Caroline Warren/Photodisc, Catherine
Delahaye/DigitalVision, Copyright Crezalyn Nerona Uratsuji/Moment,
eclipse_images/E+, FatCamera/iStock, FatCamera/iStock, FG Trade Latin/E+,
FG Trade/E+, Fly View Productions/E+, Fransje Van Riel/iStock, Gary S
Chapman/Photographer's Choice RF, Gins Wang/E+, Henrik Karlsson/
Moment, ibnjaafar/E+, Image Source/Photodisc, IndiaPix/IndiaPicture,
Iuliia Burmistrova/Moment, James O'Neil/The Image Bank, Jami Tarris/
Stone, JazzIRT/iStock, JGI/Jamie Grill/Tetra images, John W. Banagan/
Stone, Jose Luis Pelaez Inc/DigitalVision, kali9/E+, kampee patisena,
kate_sept2004/E+, kcpetersen/iStock, kool99/E+, Lane Oatey/Blue Jean
Images, Layland Masuda/Moment Open, Lisa5201/E+, M Swiet Productions/
Moment, Maskot, Mint Images, MoMo Productions/DigitalVision, Noel
Hendrickson/DigitalVision, ozgurdonmaz/E+, Peter Dazeley, Peter Dazeley/
The Image Bank, Peter Schoen/Moment, Phynart Studio/E+, pinstock/E+,
puhimec/iStock, Robert Muckley/Moment, Roberto Moiola/Sysaworld/
Moment, Ross Anania/Photodisc, Salman Ansari/iStock, Serge Melesan/
iStock, SeventyFour/iStock, ShutterRunner.com (Matty Wolin)/Moment, Shy
Al Britanni/arabianEye, Sneksy/E+, solidcolours/E+, SolStock/E+, Suwimon
Watanapanidmongkol/iStock, svetikd/E+, Thanasis Zovoilis/DigitalVision,
The Good Brigade/DigitalVision, ti-ja/iStock, Tom Werner, triloks/E+,
Tuul & Bruno Morandi, Vicki Jauron, Babylon and Beyond Photography/
Moment, vitranc/E+, Westend61, wundervisuals, xavierarnau/E+); Oxford
University Press (123rf, 123RF/Photographee.eu, Shutterstock/Christine Bird,
Shutterstock/e X p o s e, Shutterstock/Evlakhov Valeriy, Shutterstock/Leena
Robinson, Shutterstock/Lim Yong Hian, MM Studios, Shutterstock/Stephanie
Periquet, Shutterstock/Thirteen, Shutterstock/Valentin Agapov, Shutterstock/
Volodymyr Burdiak); Shutterstock (acceptphoto, Aibina Nizamova, Albina
Gavrilovic, all_about_people, Allen.G, Altsva, Andi111, AndreaMazzi, Andrei
Armiagov, Andy Shell, Andy333, Anton Watman, antoniodiaz, ANURAK
PONGPATIMET, aodaodaodaod, Athapet Piruksa, Bangkok Click Studio,
Basileus, BearFotos, Beekeepx, Bob Pool, Bonnie Taylor Barry, Brian A
Jackson, Butterfly Hunter, Catarina Belova, Catchlight Lens, cesc_assawin,
Chubykin Arkady, Dai Mar Tamarack, David Persson, Diego Barbieri,
digidreamgrafix, Dmytro Zinkevych, Dragon Images, Drazen Zigic, Ebtikar,
Ekateryna Zubal, Elena Schweitzer, Elizabeth_0102, Endika Echevarria, ESB
Professional, essevu, everydayplus, EZ-Stock Studio, Fernando Avendano,
Fiona Ayerst, fizkes, frank60, Galyna Myroniuk, gdvcom, Gorodenkoff,
Ground Picture, Hananeko_Studio, HandmadePictures, Honorable, Horse
Crazy, Hryshchyshen Serhii, hxdbzxy, idreamphoto, ifiStudio, Ines Behrens-
Kunkel, Ivan Soto Cobos, Jack Hong, Jon Nicholls Photography, jordaneil,
Joseph Hendrickson, Juliya Shangarey, Just Life, khlungcenter, Kjeld Friis,
Komuso and Colorsandia, kostasgr, Kpad, Ku_suriuri, Kuttelvaserova
Stuchelova, kwanchai.c, Ladanifer, Larry Eiden, Laura Hedien, Leena
Robinson, leungchopan, LightField Studios, Linda McKusick, Little Vignettes
Photo, Littlekidmoment, livcool, Lopolo, lovelyday12, Lubenica, manfredxy,
Manuel Findeis, MaraZe, MarcelClemens, Marianna Ianovska, Mary Luts,
Michael Conrad, Michael Potter11, Michelle Aleksa, MillaF, Monkey Business
Images, mykhailo pavlenko, NatchaS, Neo Edmund, New Africa, Nutlegal
Photographer, nuttawut ruangkijparitt, Odua Images, Oleg Kozlov, Olga
Danylenko, OlhaTsiplyar, oneinchpunch, Onjira Leibe, ORION PRODUCTION,
oTTo-supertramp, Pachai Leknettip, pamas, Patryk Kosmider, Paul Tessier,
PeopleImages.com - Yuri A, Peter Fodor, PHOTO JUNCTION, Pierre-Yves
Babelon, Pixel-Shot, poltu shyamal, Prostock-studio, Raushan_films, Retouch
man, Riaz Ul Islam, Rich Carey, Robert Kneschke, Roman Belogorodov, Roy
Babiuk, RugliG, Samuel Borges Photography, Sebastian_Photography, Sergey
Uryadnikov, showcake, Shutterstock, SlavaFlash, Sokolov Alexey, SpeedKingz,
Steve Lagreca, sweet_tomato, T.TATSU, Teresa Moore, TuktaBaby, TY Lim,
Tyler Olson, Ulmus Media, UV70, VAKS-Stock Agency, Vera Verano Photo,
VH-studio, Viorel Kurnosov, Vito Inguglia, Volha Shakhava, wavebreakmedia,
worawit_j, WtvShop, xbrchx, xtock, yadom, Yayayoyo, Yiistocking, Yuriy Kulik).